COMMUNICATION
IN PULPIT
AND PARISH

Communication in Pulpit and Parish

by MERRILL R. ABBEY

THE WESTMINSTER PRESS
Philadelphia

PUBLISHED BY THE WESTMINSTER PRESS®
PHILADELPHIA, PENNSYLVANIA

PRINTED IN THE UNITED STATES OF AMERICA

Library of Congress Cataloging in Publication Data

Abbey, Merrill R.
    Communication in pulpit and parish.

    Includes bibliographical references.
    1. Communication (Theology)   2. Preaching.
I. Title.
BV4319.A23   253   72-14329
ISBN 0-664-20967-X

To the
Chicago Christian Communications Center:
colleagues of the decade 1963–1973
in a pathfinding adventure
in ecumenical interseminary training
for the ministry of mass communication

CONTENTS

PREFACE

Any sizable current poll of seminarians or young ministers is likely to divide rather evenly between two priorities. Approximately half of such a group will stress concern for the many-faceted applications of the communication process, including preaching as one communicative ministry among others. The rest will give first place to preaching and its requisite skills, aware that a wider understanding of human communication is necessary to that end. Either concern finds its completion in the other; this book is designed to meet the needs of both.

Communication research has advanced rapidly in recent years, and its findings afford vital equipment for the minister's work in pastoral care of persons and leadership of the church in mission. These chapters seek to help the student or minister appropriate this data and orient his further studies in the literature of communication.

As a significant communication ministry, preaching requires new grounding in emerging understandings of communication as a process. For more than a decade no new book has attempted to examine the homiletic task in its wholeness; publication in the field has focused on particularized aspects of preaching. The excellent general textbooks of the 1940's and 1950's, antedating the communication revolution, could offer little access to the vistas it has opened. This book seeks to meet the need for a comprehensive examination of the field in the light of developments in the intervening years.

At an early stage in its preparation, I sought the guidance of professors of preaching and communication in theological seminaries widely distributed in both geographical setting and denominational affiliation. Their generous responses made a twofold contribution. They contributed encouragement to proceed with the task. Among a score of them, there was consensus that, as one of them put it, "there is definitely a need for a fresh approach to interpreting and presenting the new situation created by contemporary interest in communication, mass media, etc., and its relationship to the traditional homiletical discipline. This is *new* ground." Such a volume, most of them said, "is long overdue."

They also contributed a fund of insight that I might have missed but for their aid. Studying a synopsis of my original plan, many of them made valuable suggestions of matters I had not included or of ways in which better balance among emphases could be secured. All of these corrective suggestions have been carefully considered, and nearly all have resulted in modifications of the project and, I trust, in its strengthening.

For such contributions I am especially indebted to Professors V. John Bachman, San Francisco Theological Seminary; Charles H. Bayer, Chicago Theological Seminary; Louis W. Bloede and Olin M. Ivey, Evangelical Theological Seminary; Harold Brack, Drew University Theological School; Herbert J. Doran (emeritus), University of Dubuque Theological Seminary; LeRoy E. Kennel, Bethany Theological Seminary; Robert E. Luccock, Boston University School of Theology; Donald MacLeod, Princeton Theological Seminary; Wesley W. Nelson, North Park Theological Seminary; Stanley D. Schneider, Evangelical Lutheran Theological Seminary; Roy W. Seibel, North American Baptist Seminary; John Skoglund, Colgate Rochester Divinity School; Ronald Sleeth, Perkins School of Theology; and Gordon G. Thompson, Emory University, The Candler School of Theology. While they must not be held responsible for the work that has emerged and can hardly be expected to agree with all that they find here, they may take comfort in the thought that without their counsel the work would be less satisfactory than they find it.

To many others I am grateful: to congregations from whom, in more than thirty years of pastoral ministry, I learned the foundation lessons in communication; to my students and colleagues in Garrett Theological Seminary, who have stimulated and sharpened many of the insights in these pages; to researchers in the fields covered, on whose findings I have drawn; to their publishers for generous permission to quote from these materials; to Mrs. Eve Messner for the patience and enthusiasm which, through a busy summer, she invested in transforming my untidy copy into precise typescript; and to my wife, whose unfailing interest in this—as in all my work—has gone far to make of a demanding task a joy.

M.R.A.

PART ONE

Communication as Ministry

CHAPTER 1

Communication—
Basic to Ministry

Ministry, as we are coming to understand it, is almost synonymous with communication. Once a standard equivalent phrase for preaching, "communicating the gospel" no longer has that one-to-one identification. Proclamation is still a central function of the church and its ministry, but channels of communication beyond the preached word have become impressive.

Nonverbal communication—styled "body language" in one best-selling book—has won wide attention. Anthropological studies by Edward T. Hall reveal, for example, the significance of waiting time as codified in various cultures. Hall cites a diplomatic tangle occasioned by failure to recognize the variations among these codes. An American ambassador receiving official visits of welcome to his new post was incensed by the arrival of one delegation fifty minutes after the appointed time. Since on the one hand exact punctuality might be interpreted as subservience, and since on the other hand they did not wish to be disrespectful, the local diplomats had carefully timed their arrival to convey that meaning. An hour of tardiness in their culture was equivalent to five minutes in ours, their fifty minutes was equivalent to our four, their forty-five to our three. As in America we feel obligated to mutter some half-apologetic word for five minutes of tardiness, they apologized for their fifty minutes; but the new ambassador's misunderstanding of the code caused strained relations.[1]

As with waiting time, so with personal space, gesture, touching others, and many other factors, nonverbal communication
is so codified in relation to cultural context that Hall can generalize: "Culture is communication and communication is culture." [2]

In a time when a highly skilled profession has concentrated
its energies on creating public images designed to communicate
what corporations or political figures desire to say about themselves, it has become obvious that the church's image communicates something of importance concerning its message. At
least from the time of Francis of Assisi, who insisted that he
and his brother monks did their best preaching through their
life among men, Christians have been conscious of the eloquence
of actions. Now, however, with a new awareness of varying
life-styles consciously adopted and frequently changed, communication through life-style has become a matter of articulate
Christian concern. When to image and life-style are added the
new media of an electric and electronic age, the complex variety
of means of communication available to those who minister
becomes overwhelming.

Communication is more than a complex means of ministry,
of sharing the Christian faith and its liberating benefits. It also
comprises an important content of ministry. To enable persons
to communicate more freely is a prime objective of the healing
and helping professions. The speech therapist, for example,
changes more than the way a patient talks. His therapy puts
new content into the patient's conception of himself and opens
new possibilities in his relations with others. The counselor who
frees members of a troubled family to communicate with one
another past formerly inhibiting barriers may by that achievement go far toward mending the breakdown of domestic relations. The psychiatrist who opens communication with a patient's repressed and infected memories performs a healing
service. Pastoral ministry so partakes of this content of communication that it would not be far wrong, paraphrasing Hall,
to say that ministry is communication and communication is
ministry.

Communication in a Minister's Day

To see the truth of the foregoing statement, it is useful to review the log of a not unusual day in the life of a pastor. He is awakened by the pillow speaker of his bedside radio alarm clock; thus his day begins by his personally predesigned inter-action with the media of mass communication. Going immedi-ately to his study, he spends an hour in Biblical exegesis, medi-tation, and prayer (communication with the Christian tradition, with himself, with God). At breakfast with his family, he dis-cusses with them their plans for the day and formulates agree-ments concerning his participation in some of their activities (communication through dialogue). After breakfast he spends a few minutes carefully skimming the newspaper and listening to a television news roundup (communication through news media).

Returning to his study, the pastor reads a portion of a sig-nificant book (communication through print), hears an im-portant lecture recorded on cassette tape (communication through the spoken word at long range), and writes a draft of his sermon for the coming Sunday (communication through literary expression as a basis for anticipated spoken communica-tion). Before he has finished this task, he is interrupted by a telephone call. Listening to the voice over the wire, he recognizes an only partially suppressed emotion, which alters the surface meaning of the spoken words. As a result, he arranges to see the caller before the day is over (nonverbal communication by voice quality).

At lunch he meets with a committee making plans for the next steps in a project by which his congregation is attempting to meet a neglected need of its neighborhood (communication by group dynamics as part of a larger communication by sig-nificant action). He then drives to the church office in traffic controlled by stoplights and octagonal signs at some through streets (communication by symbol). On his way he waves to a colleague with whom there is no opportunity to speak in the busy traffic. The colleague, guessing his unspoken question about a shared project, holds up his right hand with thumb and fore-finger joined and supported by three upright fingers in an O.K. sign (communication by gesture).

Reaching the office, he quickly goes through his mail, which contains, in addition to a number of letters, a pamphlet dealing with an aspect of the denomination's program and a poster for display in the church building (communication by print and visual material). Responding, he dictates several letters and takes time for two handwritten notes to young people away at college and in the Armed Forces (personal communication by the written word). Before going on to the other tasks of the afternoon, he prepares copy for the church bulletin for the coming Sunday, selecting materials to be inserted in the morning liturgy and writing a brief message concerning parish activities (print media reinforcing liturgical and congregational com-munication).

The pastor then spends an hour with a couple whose marriage is in danger, listening not only to their words but to the tones of their voices, the quality of their silences, and the attitudes expressed by their body movements. When he speaks, it is less to tell them something than to elicit fuller expression on their part. At the end of the interview, he takes a little time to write a transcription of key portions of the conversation and, in so doing, catches the significance he had earlier missed in parts of the situation. In the light of this interview (communication by depth listening), he makes a note of matters to be explored in the next interview.

On his way to some parish calls, the pastor stops to have coffee with a community leader who is not a member of his congregation. Although no official ministerial function is in-volved and he has no favor to seek from this man, he has found that this kind of activity (communication by presence, listening, and concern) opens the way to relations enabling both his friend and himself to act more usefully in incidents that arise from time to time. There follow several routine calls in which nothing that seems important transpires. In some places there is no one at home. Yet in each of these instances he leaves his card with a brief, warm, personal note hastily penned on the back. Unexciting as these visits have proved, he knows by experience that this (communication by personal interest) is valued by his people and that when important matters are at stake he can be more helpful to them because of the relationship that has been established.

In the evening, the pastor preaches at a special service of his church. During the opening liturgy he baptizes (communication by sacrament) a baby presented at this service because the grandparents can be present then although they could not be present on a Sunday morning. After he has preached his sermon (communication by words, gestures, and voice tones, and by reading the cues of interest, agreement, and uncertainty on the faces of the listeners) he is approached by a young man he does not know, who says, "Although we are strangers, I think, from what I heard you say tonight, that you might be able to help me work out a matter that is getting to be too much for me to handle alone." As he makes an appointment to see the youth the next day, the minister reflects that this interchange (communication by attitude) is one important test of his preaching.

Tired from a long and crowded day, the pastor goes home and relaxes before the television screen, watching a drama and a panel show with an open line for response (communication through the arts and the observation of popular feedback). It might not be surprising if, as he prepares for bed, he muses that communication is not only the means he uses in his ministry but very largely the content of which ministry is made.

Bridging the Chasms of Culture

In a pluralistic society, communication between widely differing cultures and subcultures can go seriously awry at painful cost. Julius Fast cites such an instance. In a New York City high school a Puerto Rican girl named Livia was caught with a group

of girls who were known violators of school regulations, after
one of their delinquencies. On the basis of a questioning interview, the principal decided to suspend her, saying: "It wasn't
what she said. It was simply her attitude. There was something
sly and suspicious about her. She just wouldn't meet my eye. She
wouldn't look at me."

When parental protest in the Puerto Rican community reached
near-riot proportions, a young Puerto Rican Spanish teacher
intervened. In an interview with the principal he learned the
latter's basis for his judgment of guilt and was able to explain
an important cultural fact. "In Puerto Rico a nice girl, a good
girl," he said, "does not meet the eyes of an adult. Refusing
to do so is a sign of respect and obedience. It would be as difficult for Livia to look you in the eyes as it would be for her to
misbehave, or for her mother to come to you with a complaint.
In our culture, this is just not accepted behavior for a respectable
family."

Beginning with this cross-cultural insight, it was possible to
work the matter out, save Livia from what would have been a
grave injustice, and begin the building of better relations between
the school and its neighborhood.[3]

Beyond such cross-cultural ministries in society, there are
communication needs of a more internal nature. The widespread
malady of uncertainty as to who we are is an expression of the
need for internal self-communication, traditionally known as
meditation. It is also linked to inadequate communication with
any sustaining tradition, many members of a "now generation"
having lost the ability to draw upon and identify with a meaningful past. As one aspect of this uprootedness from a tradition,
many persons complain that they cannot draw upon the resources of the Bible as the taproot of Christian insight and
faith. People need help if they are to communicate with this
spiritual heritage across the gap of centuries of time and widely
differing cultural orientations.

To meet these basic human needs for communication—in
marriage and other intimate personal relations; in congregations,

denominations, and the ecumenical fellowship; among the cultural segments of society; and between individuals and their spiritual heritage—is an important purpose of Christian ministry. For this basic content of the minister's calling, skill in the complex task of communication is a prime essential.

Theory Guides Practice

Like other skills, communication is learned only by diligent practice. Yet practice must be guided by intelligent understanding of the process on which it is based. This book is designed to provide such guidance.

In Part One, we shall examine basic elements in communication, beginning with an overview of it, not as a static affair in which one participant delivers "a communication" to another, but as a dynamic process in which there is continuous interaction. After Chapter 2 has reviewed the total process, successive chapters in Part One will deal in greater detail with interaction as the essential element, with some analytical methods of understanding those with whom we communicate, and with a discriminating approach to contemporary communications media.

Although preaching is no longer to be viewed as exclusively synonymous with "communicating the Christian message," it holds a place of such importance in Christian ministry as to call for special attention. It is a central task to which the church is commissioned by its Lord. It is understood by the church to be a primary function of its ordained ministers. It can take many and varied forms, and as media are multiplied its opportunities are not limited, but extended. It is a demanding and complex process and cannot be effectively carried out without carefully detailed understanding. For these reasons, in Part Two of this book, "Communicative Proclamation," insights derived from the study of the communication process will be applied to the ministry of preaching.

We shall begin with an assessment of what preaching can and cannot hope to accomplish in a society of many media. In the light of this, we shall consider what the role of preaching can usefully be in relation to other communication channels. We shall study what the preacher's varied tasks (as Bible interpreter, teacher, counselor, and worship celebrant) can teach us. We shall then follow through the steps in the preparation of a sermon: deriving and refining the creative idea, working out the design that will best meet the needs of real communication, entering into an interactive relation in which the listener becomes a creative participant in the preaching situation, finding and using materials that have power to communicate with clarity and force, expressing the message in a style that speaks authentically for the preacher as a whole person, delivering the message in a way that meets real needs of the listener, and doing all this work by methods that can stimulate continuous growth in the minister as an effective communicator and person.

PROBES

One axiom of our subject holds that little communication occurs unless both source and receiver are active in the process. To help to make the reader's relation to the contents of this book more profitably active, we shall include a few "probes" at the end of each chapter. Sometimes these will suggest ways to probe the material by further reading. Sometimes they will indicate thought probes that may be pursued, sometimes practical applications.

1. Log your own activities for a day, noting the ways in which communication is involved. What successes of the day are influenced by useful communication? Where communication fails, what are the consequences? Can you discover any of the reasons for these communication failures?

2. Describe the life of the church you know best, in terms of its flow of communication. Who communicates with whom? By what means? What blocks to communication can you discover? Are there any aspects of this church's ministry that cannot be described in terms of communication? How does this

church communicate with the community outside its membership? Can the communication it has with those outside be described as ministry? By what criteria can you estimate the effects of such communication? In the light of these criteria, how effective is it?

CHAPTER 2

Understanding
the Communication Process

The term "a communication" can mislead us. It suggests
something finished and closed, as if a commodity were passed
from source to receiver. Yet what transpires is a *process* in
which source and receiver interact more or less imperfectly in
arriving at some degree of common understanding.

Between "a communica*tion*" and the process of "communicat*ing*" the difference can be dramatic. An example from history
will illustrate this difference. A generation ago the George Arliss
film *House of Rothschild* made major use of an incident that
occurred at the end of the Napoleonic wars. In the dots and
dashes of powerful light beams, a message flashed across the
English Channel brought the dire news, "Wellington defeated."
Among other consequences, a disastrous financial panic swept
the British Board of Trade. No error or duplicity had been involved in the sending of the news. As actually transmitted it
said, "Wellington defeated Napoleon at Waterloo." A proper
communication had been sent, but fog sweeping in had oblit-
erated all but the first two words, leaving a tragic hiatus between
"a communica*tion*" and the process of communicat*ing*.

A wry remark by Woodrow Wilson brought the difference
still closer to the immediate experience of many readers. An
interviewer, alluding to Wilson's long experience as a college
professor before his entrance into politics, asked what had

been the strongest impression he brought from his teaching career. "My strongest impression," the President replied, "is that of the infinite capacity of the human mind to resist information."

We shall not comment on Wilson as an educator (the remark was obviously whimsical and at least half facetious). But the force of the remark rests on a conception of education as bundled information communicated by teacher to student. Progress in learning is in no small part a long struggle to move from such a static model (in which the student often does resist information!) to one of interaction, which involves the student as one who takes initiative in discovery and in which student and teacher are learners together. Every such advance moves a little from instruction as "a communic*ation*" to shared learning as communic*ating*.

Communication as a Process

So common is this double meaning of the term "communication" that dictionaries which carefully report how words are used call attention to both meanings. *Webster's Seventh New Collegiate Dictionary,* for instance, gives a series of definitions, of which the first reads: "an act or instance of transmitting." Reading this, one remembers the classroom lecture detailing a wealth of information, some major portion of which is "resisted." One recalls the transmission "Wellington defeated Napoleon at Waterloo." It is not until the fifth definition in the series that the dictionary reports: "a process by which meanings are exchanged between individuals through a common system of symbols." Yet the implications of this last definition open the doors to the most profitable study of communication in ministry.

Several aspects of this dynamic definition are important to our thought. (*a*) It suggests that communication is not a completed entity passed from one party to another, but an exchange

of meanings between two parties. We shall have occasion to
return to this idea more than once in subsequent chapters. (*b*)
The definition refers to a common system of symbols. The use
of a common system of symbols or signals for communication
will loom large in our consideration of encoding, decoding, channels, and media. (*c*) For our overall understanding of communication, the term "process" holds major significance.

A process is dynamic, not static. "A communication" (e.g.,
"Wellington defeated . . .") fails because it is static. In the film
House of Rothschild, the Rothschilds have devised a highly developed system of exchange of information via carrier pigeons,
and because of the dynamics of this network they are successful
in communica*ting* in ways that save the market from complete
collapse. We shall see that such exchange of meanings is crucial
to a communicative ministry.

Two aspects of communication viewed as a process become
vital in our study. (*a*) Seeing communication as a process, we
look at it in terms of continuous change, not only in the transaction between participants but in the transaction within the
participants themselves. (*b*) Communication viewed as a process
is seen as a continuous interplay among the elements in the
situation—not only between sender and receiver but among the
successive or simultaneous behaviors of each as the process unfolds. Other elements besides fog rolling in after the transmission
of the first two words of a message can block the exchange of
meanings, and any useful study of communication must seek to
identify and deal with these portions of the process.

Ministry can be seriously impeded, even defeated, by the
notion that the minister's principal role is that of "telling" others
something he can "give" them. Honest introspection will convince most of us that we have received valuable influence from
those who were open to be influenced by us. One who ministers
has learned important elements of truth, which he seeks to
share. Few thoughtful ministers would suppose, however, that
their truth is complete, or that they are infallible, or that those
to whom they minister have nothing to teach. Even in areas

where our knowledge is far advanced over that of others, we are best able to share our meanings when we have listened to others' meanings and are therefore able to relate our meanings to theirs.

Failures at this point underlie the accusation, often heard, that ministers spend too much time answering questions nobody is asking. Ministers who address themselves to questions others urgently raise find a ready ear for their communications and a sure response to them.

In this chapter we will look more closely at communication as a process, beginning with Aristotle's early perception and proceeding to two currently influential formulations. Later chapters will study parts of the process in fuller detail, but first we need a panoramic view of the major process.

The Aristotelian Triad

Stemming from Aristotle's *Rhetoric,* a classic conception of the process has fixed attention on three elements: speaker, speech, and audience. This useful triad has guided the study of public address and homiletics over the years. It suggests that attention can be fixed on the speech itself in order to study its parts, its organization, its deriving and handling of information, its illustration, its motivating factors, and many other characteristics. At other times it fixes attention on the audience and by audience analysis helps the speaker to find his target.

Yet again, it studies the speaker himself. For example, one analysis of the speaker, based on this triad, finds the keys to effectiveness in good character (we listen most readily to those we believe to be trustworthy), good will (we are most open to the ideas of those who seem to respect us), good sense (we are most persuaded by matter that seems to hold together sensibly and to square with the rest of what we know), concern for the other's mind (new meanings cannot reach us unless they connect with meanings we already have), and use of the other's language (we can understand the speaker only if he uses words and sym-

bols that mean to us something closely similar to what they
mean to him).[1]

Important areas of concern for communication in ministry
are thus made accessible for study through the Aristotelian
triad. Yet without great care this conception of the speech almost as a missile hurled at an audience by a speaker can miss
important dynamics of the process. To fix attention on these
dynamic elements, various other models have been devised.

The Shannon-Weaver Model

One of these communication models is widely known as the
Shannon-Weaver model. Claude E. Shannon, who with Warren
Weaver prepared the paper setting it forth, was associated with
the Bell Telephone Laboratories. Coming out of research so
based, this model was freed from the speaker-speech-audience
triad by its involvement with communication in a wider context.
Originally designed to study what goes on in the technological
media of communication themselves, it attracted the attention
of students of human communication as a flexible scheme for
exposing elements of the process important to them.

As shown in Figure 1, the Shannon-Weaver model [2] deals
with five elements of the communication process: a source from
which a message emanates, a transmitter that encodes the message, a signal that carries it, a receiver that decodes the message,
and a destination to which the message is directed. The encoding
transmitter, the signal, and the decoding receiver together constitute the medium—telephone, radio, newspaper, the spoken
word, or one of the many other possible media. Several links in

Figure 1. The Shannon-Weaver Model

the communicative process that were not apparent in the simpler Aristotelian design now come into view. We shall look briefly at each of these.

For purposes of our study of communication in ministry, the source is personal. In other words, the source is the individual (or institution or group) that initiates the process. The source has a need or purpose which the communication is intended to help to fulfill. The source determines what message will best serve this purpose, selects the destination, or party to whom it will be directed, and chooses the medium that is to be used. Knowing that a message carried by more than one medium has a greater probability of being understood, he may elect to use some combination of media. For example, he might decide to preach a sermon reinforced with slides and a taped interview, or to send a message through a parish newsletter followed by calls from a telephone task force. These choices made by the source, together with the skill he brings to them, are important in the study of communication.

Encoding the message begins the process of making it available to the destination. This may mean putting it into words. The problem will then be to find words that are capable of saying all that the source intends, words that will be understood without mistake by the destination. This will involve choice of language, dialect, and idiom familiar to the destination. It will require a language level that is neither so technical (or literary) as to be meaningless to the destination nor so elementary as to incur his resistance by seeming to talk down to him. In addition to using words—or possibly instead of using words—the source may decide to encode his message in nonverbal acts, pictures, or banner symbols; or to use print or radio instead of direct address. With each of these choices a new range of encoding problems will appear.

The signal is the beam of directed energy that carries the encoded message: electrical, as in the instance of telephone, radio, or television; or mechanical, as in the case of lungs, larynx, resonating chambers, tongue, and lips, which generate the sound

waves in face-to-face speech. There are times when studied
control of these signal energies must have focused attention, but
we need not linger over them in our present view of the total
process.

The destination must be able to decode what the source has
encoded. In parts of Africa, for example, the attractiveness of
television as a means of communicating needed information concerning national development, literacy, or the gospel, must be
countered by the fact that there are very few television receivers
available. While radio may be less capable of carrying all that
one would like to convey in picture and word, it is the better
medium in such regions because almost the entire population
has access to radio receivers. Or, to change the example, in
some parishes a message encoded in banners, folk music, and
multimedia devices that speak warmly to young people has been
so difficult for their elders to decode as to seem to be alien to
the gospel or perhaps to subvert it entirely. How to encode a
message in such a way that those for whom it is intended can
accurately decode it must be a constant concern of communicative ministry.

The destination of the communication is any one of the many
intended audiences: one's wife across the breakfast table, the
patient visited in a hospital, other members of a committee with
whom one works, a child in a confirmation class, the alderman
whose vote on a civil rights issue is in question, or the Sunday
morning congregation. Whether helpful communication occurs
will depend on the ability of source and destination to put themselves in each other's role and to answer such questions as: What
is he trying to say? What would I be trying to say if I were in
his place? When he uses that word, what does he mean by it?
Does it mean to him what it means to me? To get answers to
these and many other such questions, the source must sensitively
study the destination. Such study is another vital area of growth
toward greater competency in communicating.

Thus the Shannon-Weaver model has suggested ways in which
analysis of the source, the encoding transmitter, the signal, the

decoding receiver, and the destination can increase our understanding and facilitate our use of the communicative process.

The SMCR Model

The so-called SMCR model (see Figure 2) was devised by David K. Berlo.[3] It provides a means for probing the communication process in still further detail. Such examination is the purpose for which various models are designed. There is no intention to say: This is what communication *is*. S. I. Hayakawa has warned us that words are "maps" and not the "territories" themselves. They *represent* things or events, but they are not themselves the things represented. As Hayakawa points out, many of our difficulties in human relations are the product of confusing the word-map with the thing-territory. This distinction applies equally to models of the communication process.

Figure 2. Berlo's SMCR Model

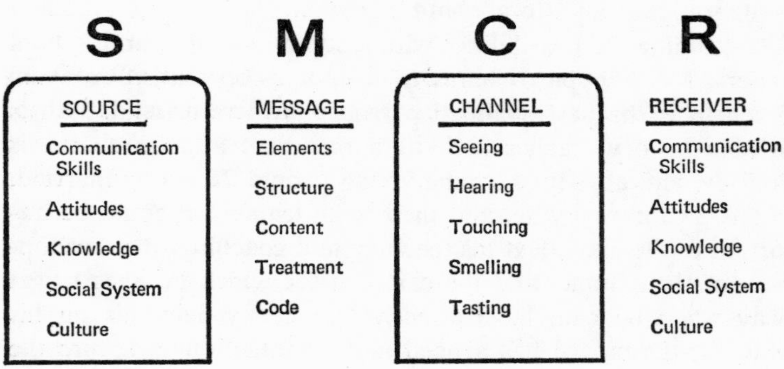

S	M	C	R
SOURCE	MESSAGE	CHANNEL	RECEIVER
Communication Skills	Elements	Seeing	Communication Skills
Attitudes	Structure	Hearing	Attitudes
Knowledge	Content	Touching	Knowledge
Social System	Treatment	Smelling	Social System
Culture	Code	Tasting	Culture

Models serve their purpose when they isolate elements or relationships in the process in ways that contribute to fruitful study. In this book we use a number of different models to enable us to examine various parts of the process. Berlo's SMCR model helps us to see the interacting parts of the process in ways that can advance our study materially at this point.

Some differences from the Shannon-Weaver model become evident at a glance. Berlo's model is designed for the study of human communication, as distinguished from technological communication. The Shannon-Weaver source and transmitter are elided into Berlo's source, who encodes. Similarly the Shannon-Weaver receiver and destination become Berlo's receiver, who decodes. The Shannon-Weaver signal becomes the Berlo channel, which must make contact with one or more of the senses. It may be helpful to look at a simple incident in ministry through the lens of Berlo's "source-message-channel-receiver" model.

The SMCR Model Applied

The Rev. Ernest Sheppard, facing a vacancy in the teaching of a potentially vigorous class of junior high youth, is concerned to enlist for the post someone who by training and personal qualifications will be adequate for, and measure up to, the strategic opportunity. His motivating need triggers his activity as the source in a pastoral communication.

Examining the possibilities with a committee of church school leaders, Mr. Sheppard shares their conclusion that young Will Teachem is the best-qualified person anywhere around. Will is an able history teacher and, as a part-time athletic coach, is liked by, and attractive to, the young people. Not long married, he has a charming wife, and their team leadership could be important to the class. But his teaching and coaching, the development of their home, and the camping for which he likes to get away when he can, have already laid heavy demands on his time. Mr. Sheppard has a need and an intention to secure the services of Will Teachem, but how shall he encode his message?

He thinks carefully about Will's interests and how he can appeal to them. He ponders how best to beam his message to the younger man's sense of worth and his dedication as a Christian. But as he plans the interview he wonders if these verbal appeals will be enough. Perhaps he should encode his message through more than one channel. Would some nonverbal communication help? How would it be if he were to take Dr. Layman with him on the call, to show Will that this matter is not just the minister's hobby but the concern of respected and busy people of the congregation? That, he tells himself, would be a good way to get the message across. So he enlists Dr. Layman's help and makes the appointment with Will.

In the interview, Will Teachem must decode the message. What these men are asking is clear enough, but what do they really mean? Is the job as easy as they make it appear? If so, couldn't any one of a dozen or more other people do it just as well? Are they really concerned about the youth or about filling a vacant slot in the organization chart? Why did these two older men come to see him—are they trying to manipulate him by this appeal to his ego? Why did Mr. Sheppard bring Dr. Layman and not some of the members of the class? Don't the youngsters have any voice in the matter?

Mr. Teachem may finally say Yes or No to the invitation, but in the process he must work his way through such questions as these. In doing so he will initiate his own communications with his visitors, encode his own messages; when he does, the process becomes a lively dialogue of give-and-take.

When the communication is done, its success or failure will have turned on many factors. Mr. Sheppard may have been wise or mistaken in his original message and the way he encoded it. The nonverbal message conveyed by involving Dr. Layman may have been useful or may have misfired because, rightly or wrongly, Will Teachem read it as a patronizing gesture.

As a receiver, Will may have been an attentive listener who could put himself in his callers' position, who understood their concerns; or he may have been preoccupied with other interests that blocked their message from really getting through. He may even have felt an inner antagonism because of conflicting images in his mind. Troubled with some personal problems and needing help from such men, who might be personally concerned for him, he may have read their attitude as expressing a greater desire to use than to help him.

The level of effectiveness in communicating could thus have been advanced or blocked at many points in the process. We can discern these points more accurately by scrutinizing the four concepts of the SMCR model in this order: source, receiver, message, and channel.

Factors Affecting the Source

Numerous factors influence the source's effectiveness in communication:

1. The source's *communication skills* are important—his use of language and other encoding devices (such as his writing style or his adeptness in the use of visual materials or other media), and his capacity to put himself in the receiver's place and enter empathically into a genuine relationship with him.

2. The *attitudes* of the source color all that transpires in the process. His attitude toward the receiver—whether he presses his communication aggressively, is hesitant and obsequious, or is quietly confident and approachable—goes far toward opening or restricting the communicative relationship between them. His attitudes toward himself and his message are similarly significant. Is he at peace with himself? Does he have confidence in his message and in his own ability to deliver it? Or is he apologetic and fearful on the one hand, seemingly arrogant on the other?

3. The source's *knowledge* conditions his success. In ministry, this involves his understanding of persons and the deeper springs of their being, his knowledge of the Christian message and its Biblical and theological sources, his knowledge of human affairs and the individual and social ethics that guide them, and his commonsense judgment about everyday life. Other factors can hardly give effective weight to his communication in the absence of such basic knowledge.

4. The communication takes place within a *social system,* and the relation of the source to this system further colors his effectiveness. Within the group in which he and the receiver are placed, what is the position of the source? Does he occupy a

place of respect? Is he in harmony with the group or at odds with it? In ministry, is he fulfilling the role expectations of the church and its people? As some students of parish ministry analyze the situation, ministers who desire to press innovative activities and programs "pay their rent" on their leadership by effectiveness in traditional roles: preaching, calling, pastoral care, and management of the institution. Having fulfilled these "rent-paying" roles, they are free to create the other ministerial roles important to them, with full acceptance by the parish. If these role expectations are not fulfilled, however, all their other attempts at communicative ministries labor under serious handicap.[4]

5. Not only is the source related to particular organizational structures, such as the local parish, the denomination, and social systems within the local community; he communicates within the framework of the total *cultural system* of which he is a part, and his communication must be harmonious with standards set by the culture.

Factors Involving the Receiver

Because communication is not a commodity finished and delivered by the source, but an interacting process, these same factors of skill, attitude, knowledge, and relation to the social system and the wider cultural system apply equally to the receiver. Although, for purposes of study, we analyze the receiver separately, it is important to remember that the functions of source and receiver are carried on simultaneously and are in constant interplay. Either participant in the process may be at the same time both a source and a receiver.

For instance, the minister in the act of preaching encodes a message for which he is the source; but in the process he decodes, by exegesis and hermeneutical study, a Biblical message for which he is the receiver. As he preaches, he encodes his message in words, gestures, facial expressions, tonal qualities of his voice. But even while he does so, the quality of his communication is enhanced by the skill with which he decodes messages that are coming back to him from the people through their facial expressions, the direction of their gaze, their body posture and movements, and a host of other cues, which the skilled communicator must learn to read. To separate source and receiver in any substantive sense is false to the situation and can be justified only as an analytical device for the purpose of more careful study.

For that purpose it is useful to note what the receiver brings to the process:

1. The receiver brings his own *skills* in listening, catching the key idea or ideas of a communication, intelligently reading a written or printed message, sharing a situation with enough empathy to think with another person, etc.

2. He brings his own *attitudes,* e.g., openness and interest, withdrawal, antagonism, boredom.

3. He brings his own *knowledge* of subjects discussed, the meanings he attaches to key concepts and to words and symbols used, the blanks in his knowledge, and his preconceptions, which either advance or impede the communication.

4. Like the source, the receiver is part of a *social system* in terms of immediate groups to which he belongs.

5. He lives within and is conditioned by a wider *cultural system*. In a pluralistic society, source and receiver may have their basic identifications with differing cultures or subcultures. When this is true, the fact calls for careful attention. (Note the example of Livia in Chapter 1.)

Study of the role of the receiver is important to one who ministers. The effective minister spends much of his time and energy in listening and in other receiver roles. Attention to his development as a sensitive receiver is vital to his usefulness. Furthermore, when he serves as source, his only useful objective is to establish an open communicative relationship with his receiver and to achieve a clear and effective exchange of meanings with him. To accomplish this purpose, it is essential that, as the source, he achieve understanding of the receiver's level of skills, his attitudes, something of what he knows and does not know about the matters at issue, and his affiliations within a social-cultural environment.

A Message and Its Channel

What passes between source and receiver is a message (or messages). This requires analytical attention. A message has *elements*—the parts that compose it: words, sentences, ideas; pictures or other visual content; musical elements; and the like. A message may also be viewed in terms of its *structure*—the organizational relationships in which these elements are brought together. These are the formal aspects of the study of a message.

But a message may also be considered in terms of its content, code, and treatment. In Part Two our study of communicative proclamation will return to these matters in some detail. The study of sermon *content* asks insistent questions about its central, dynamic idea: How tightly is the idea formulated? Is the idea adequately embodied in basic supportive information? The *encoding* of the sermon is a matter of finding accurate, persuasive language to express it and of giving it further clarification in fitting illustrative matter and other symbolizations, perhaps including apt use of other media in some combination with the spoken word of direct address. *Treatment* is the term used to cover the whole complex of decisions that have to be made about content, structure, delivery, and personal style in the communication.

Consideration of the channel of communication can be simplified for present purposes to a recognition that the source is always faced with the problem of what channel or channels may be most appropriately employed for the particular message he has to convey at the time. What will be the effect on exactly this message if it is conveyed by telephone instead of a personal call? What different effects would result from putting it into a letter? When does a sermon serve best, and when is a discussion a better channel? For what purposes would it be better to use some combination of the two? With these and many similar channel questions we shall need to deal in subsequent chapters.

At this point it is sufficient to note that most messages in a communicative ministry involve some combination of channels, as the model in Figure 3 may help us to see.[5] Channel 1 might be the spoken sermon in a church service, Channel 2 the nonverbal communications of the minister, and Channel 3 the architectural setting.

Figure 3. Multiple Channels

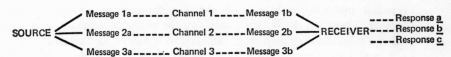

Suppose the spoken sermon were to deal with God's loving care of his children as expressed through the dependable providences of an orderly world. What might be the effect of that message, coming through Channel 1, if the nonverbal communications on Channel 2 carried a message through a strained facial expression, nervously fidgety gestures, and a vocal tone made high and harsh by a throat tense with anxiety? What other effects might follow from still another message over Channel 3, in the form of bulletins from the preceding week still left in some of the pews, numbers off center on the hymn board, and a pulpit or altar frontal hanging askew? For how many worshipers could the responses to the messages on the three channels be separated? For how many would the response to the sermon spoken on Channel 1 be greatly modified by the mixture of messages from Channels 2 and 3?

It is quite probable that for many receivers Message 1a, sent by the source (telling of God's loving care expressed through dependable providences in an orderly world) would be so altered by Message 2a (evidences of the source's anxiety) and Message 3a (disorder in the architectural surroundings) that Message 1b (i.e., Message 1a as decoded by the receiver) would fall far short of the clear teaching of God's love that the source had intended. Response a, then, might be something far different from the loving trust for which the words of Message 1a had called, since Response a is almost certain to be greatly influenced by Responses b and c.

An old novel, portraying with fine psychological insight the ministry of an Episcopal priest, depicts one moving scene in which a young man on his way to commit suicide boards a commuter train for his last journey. Not yet fully decided on his course, hoping that he may yet find light on his problem that will open some alternative, he sees a vacant seat available next to a man in clerical garb and, out of numerous empty places in the car, selects that one. The clerical collar has encoded a message over Channel 1 to the effect that here is a man who by vocation and training might be prepared to understand and possibly to help.

But there are other channels. The priest is busily reading what seems to be an important book, and this message coming over Channel 2 says that he is a thoughtful and probably a learned man, but that he is very busy. As the troubled young man hesitantly slips into the vacant seat, the priest does not look up. Nor does he respond to the sighs and nervous movements of his diffident seatmate. Through nearly an hour in which they ride together, he takes no notice of the young man, and this message conveyed by Channel 3 seems to the potential suicide to say so plainly that no one cares, and there is no help for him, that at the end of the ride he carries through his previously half formed plan to take his own life. The disagreement among messages on the three channels had defeated a potentially important ministry and cost a life.

Summary

In the foregoing pages we have examined the implications of a view of communication as a dynamic process in which there is continuous change and interaction between the participants and among the elements in their communicative behavior. In order to study this process, we looked at three models that analyze and symbolize the process from different points of view.

In the Aristotelian model we saw some ways of profiting by study of speaker, speech, and audience, but we noted that this model omits elements to which others direct attention.

One of those others is the Shannon-Weaver model, which examines source, encoder, signal, receiver, and destination. About this model we noted, among other things, its understanding of a medium as a coherent relationship among encoder, signal, and decoder, and we saw the role of the source as that of not only devising the message but also selecting the destination to which it is to be directed and choosing the medium most appropriate for the purpose.

We then turned to Berlo's SMCR model for further help in understanding the process. This led to an analysis of both source and receiver in their interlocking roles, each of which needs to be studied in terms of communication skills, attitudes, knowledge, and their respective placing within a social system and a more inclusive culture. We saw that messages can be studied in terms of their elements, structure, content, code, and treatment, observing that these categories will become important in later chapters. We closed our review of the process by examining the proposition that most messages in ministry are conveyed by some complex combination of simultaneous channels, and we raised questions about the effects of agreement or disharmony among the contents of these channels.

Throughout this chapter we have had repeated occasions to refer to interaction between participants in the communication process, but our models have not called specific attention to this aspect of the matter. Interaction is so essential an element of communication, however, that in the next chapter we will seek the help of other models in giving it the attention it requires.

PROBES

1. In the study of the communication incident involving the Rev. Ernest Sheppard and his parishioner, Will Teachem, a pastoral incident is described in terms of the SMCR model. Using an incident you have had opportunity to observe closely, make a similar analysis of what happened, applying the SMCR model as your method of description.

2. To supplement your reading on the process concepts, you will find basic help in the following texts: David K. Berlo, *The Process of Communication: An Introduction to Theory and Practice* (Holt, Rinehart & Winston, Inc., 1960); B. F. Jackson, Jr., ed., *Communication—Learning for Churchmen* (Communication for Churchmen series, Vol. I; Abingdon Press, 1968); and in a book of somewhat different orientation: Theodore Clevenger and Jack Matthews, *The Speech Communication Process* (Scott, Foresman & Company, 1971).

CHAPTER 3

Sharing the Essential Interaction

Communication is more than information. Information, a columnist observed, is "telling people what you think they ought to know." By contrast, communication effects interchange with what "they want to know or need to know in order to perform their tasks well." [1]

Some painful reflections from the journal of the country's largest communications company support the comparison. The *Bell Telephone Magazine,* speaking of the company's failing attempts to communicate with its corporate population of one million people, said:

"We of all companies should be the case history of successful internal communications. No other business has so much communication paraphernalia, technology and expertise at its command, and probably no other business spends so much time, thought and money filling pipelines of corporate communications media.

"Yet as we look around us . . . the evidence is frighteningly consistent that—as is the case with every other large organization—there is a difference between information and communication. Our employee body, at all levels, seems . . . more confused, more misinformed, more distrustful, more alienated than ever. Furthermore, as we have grown in size, in numbers of people and complexity of work, this communications gap has geometrically widened." [2]

These frank self-evaluations suggest that "filling pipelines," however sophisticated, is not enough. It achieves no communication that closes gaps of confusion and alienation. In a closing sentence, the report said, "There's a view that top executives and those below speak a different language, that each is tuned in to something quite different." The learning of any language is as much a matter of the ear as the tongue. Acquiring right diction in a foreign language is difficult, not only because the tongue must be trained to new muscular habits, but also because the ear must be reattuned to hear the unaccustomed accents. When, across any communication gap, people "speak a different language," the problem is not merely that of learning the right things to say; it involves hearing the other with accuracy.

This sensitivity in the essential interdependence of communication on levels significant for ministry calls for concentrated attention in this chapter.

Seven Levels of Communication

Communication may proceed at various levels of adequacy.[3] The most superficial is that of *transmission*. The huge corporation, using advanced media and expert personnel to funnel information to its employees, has no lack at the transmission level. Yet more is needed, if its people are not to remain "more confused, more misinformed, more distrustful . . . than ever." Watching the flow of transmission among the agencies of a large church denomination, and observing the numbers of confused, misinformed, sometimes alienated members, one comes to see that the problem is not limited to the business and industrial sectors. Even within the limits of a neighborhood parish the insufficiency of pure transmission becomes painfully clear.

From transmission we move to the second level, *contact*. Although this is an advance, source and receiver may remain far apart in their understandings and sympathies. The message is received. People hear the lecture, read the news release, tune in the program, see the poster. Yet little may happen in response. If there is only contact, nothing of that little is known to the source. The response may be agreement, apathy, or resentful disagreement; the source, not knowing, is in no position to adapt further transmission to the need. Confusion may multiply, distance may widen.

For this reason, the third level, *feedback,* is a vital one. We shall look further at this phenomenon later in this chapter; it will serve our present need to say that feedback is hearing (or otherwise receiving) the response to a message in such a way as to influence our further transmission. Thus feedback is important to the source in adapting transmission to the receiver's needs. It enhances the effectiveness of the source, and it is important to the receiver as a means of eliciting from the source a more useful and better understood message.

The fourth level of communication is *comprehension.* Before much useful communication can occur, a receiver must understand what a source is transmitting. The importance of feedback in achieving comprehension is illustrated in a situation familiar to all automobile drivers. Late for an engagement in a strange city, one drives into a filling station and asks directions. The desired address is not far away, as the crow flies, but getting there involves a loop around railroad yards or some other barrier, complicated by a pattern of one-way streets. The driver listens to the directions, sure he has fixed them in mind as they proceed. With a hasty "Thank you," he is on his tardy way. Following what he thought he heard, he makes a wrong turn and involves himself in a needless and frustrating detour that, with a few moments more for feedback, he might have avoided. Repeating the directions as he heard them, he might have been stopped by his guide's correction: "No, that isn't what I said. At that point you go . . . ." As in highway directions, so in all communication, comprehension needs the corrective of feedback.

Acceptance, the fifth level of communication, draws source and receiver appreciably nearer together. Full agreement is not necessarily the objective; disagreement can be healthy and a means of growth for both source and receiver. Yet some element of acceptance is essential as, contesting content, they accept one another as persons. Presumably, however, communication in ministry seeks some acceptance of the message itself. In achieving this, we are concerned with the "good sense" of the message —its factual credibility, logical structure, and motivational appeals. Nevertheless, if acceptance is to take place, more than a convincing message is required.

As we saw in Chapter 2, the receiver's social system and culture are important ingredients in the communication event. Let us translate this into a concrete situation illustrated in Figure 4. Suppose the source to be a minister seeking to influence his people toward a more open stand on minority housing in their residential neighborhood. His message is sociologically accurate, theologically sound, humanly moving. Yet the parishioner who must make up his mind about signing the petition, joining the march, or persuading his alderman, must deal with other questions: If I do this, how will my family re-

Figure 4. The Influence of Primary Groups

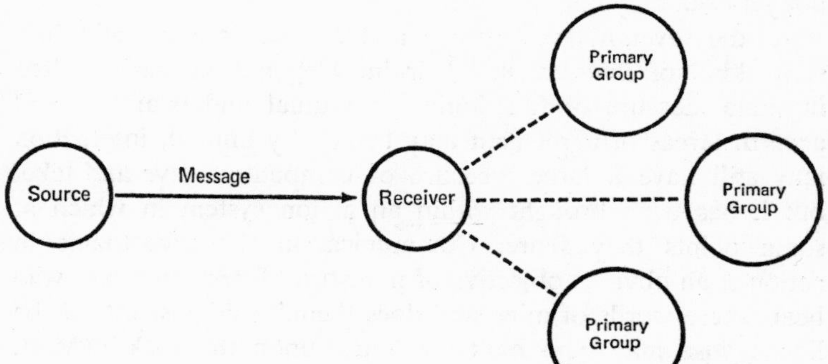

spond? Will this complicate my relationship with my wife? What will my bowling teammates say? Can I take the gaff in my car pool? For these are his primary groups in the social system that affects him as receiver. Furthermore, they take on some of their coloration from the suburban, blue-collar, or small-town culture of which they are a part. Acceptance can be achieved only within this vitally influential framework and must deal with it.

Source and receiver are brought still nearer together when communication moves to the sixth level, *internalization.* Intellectual acceptance may not deeply alter inner attitudes. Men may change the ideas they articulate about race, for example, while their slips of the tongue and nonverbal expressions betray an inward lack of commitment to the new rational structure. In a perceptive interview a Chicago workingman was quoted in observations shrewdly based on this inner division. "The average white person," he said, "you ask him about integration, is the Negro equal? He wants to scream NO. But he thinks back and he's a Christian. Now he knows in his heart that he doesn't believe he's equal, but all this Christian training almost forces him to say yes. He's saying yes to a lie, but he has to come face-to-face with the truth someday." [4] Though his statement may have reflected the man's own negative attitudes on the issue, he could support it by much data drawn from dealings with persons whose intellectual assent to Christian teaching had not yet been fully internalized.

At the seventh level, source and receiver are brought into some kind of *interaction.* Their interdependence has resulted in some measure of functioning in mutual understanding and accord. Areas of agreement may be strictly limited, interaction may still have a large measure of competitive give-and-take, but it has been brought within an action system in which at some points they share. Communication that eventuates in action is an obvious objective of ministry. "Every one then who hears these words of mine and does them," said Jesus, "will be like a wise man who built his house upon the rock" (Matt. 7:24). Again he said, "If you know these things, blessed are you if you do them" (John 13:17). Even internalization falls short of its goal until it finds expression in action.

Feedback—the Vital Link

Among the levels in the foregoing analysis, feedback forms a link so crucial as to call for separate examination. We first characterized it as hearing (or otherwise receiving) the response to a message in such a way as to influence further transmission. Technological uses of feedback can now amplify this understanding. We have feedback when part of the energy output of a technological system is put back into the system in a way to influence its future action. The howl produced in a public-address system, when volume is turned too high or one of the speakers is too close to the microphone, is a case in point. The system is rebroadcasting some of its own output, thus affecting its own operations. Most automatic devices operate on the feedback principle.

It is so in communication, where source and receiver are interdependent parts of one communication system. Part of the energy of the message is translated into cues, both verbal and nonverbal. When read by a communicator who is sensitive to his role in the interaction, these cues help him to correct his transmissions in such a way as to make them more useful to the receiver. If a feedback circuit were introduced into the Shannon-Weaver model, it might take the form shown in Figure 5. The source encodes a message, which is carried by a signal, decoded, and thus received by the destination. But, if communication is to pass beyond the level of transmission or contact, the destination must feed back some message: agreement, disagreement, question, confusion, uncertainty, restatement of the point as understood (or possibly misunderstood). The source is then able to adapt the message to the indicated need, and the communication continues in this adjusted form, indicated in the diagram by the dashed lines. In the course of an exchange of communications under conditions of useful inter-

action, there would be a long series of such adjustments, which
would call for a long receding line of dashed figures.

Figure 5. Feedback as a Continuous Process

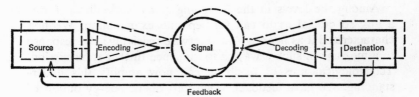

As we have noted, most interpersonal communication is
carried simultaneously on several verbal and nonverbal channels. Feedback, as a consequence, responds to the combined
effects of multiple channel messages and may itself employ several channels. Figure 6 portrays this total interaction.[5]

The counseling pastor, the teacher, or the preacher encodes
his message in various ways: words spoken in the interview,
lesson, or sermon; gestures, facial expressions, or other actions;
effects produced by rate of speech, degree of loudness or intensity of tone. As indicated by the dashed lines that tie together the arrows in Figure 6, these messages on the verbal and
nonverbal channels are sent and received as interconnected parts
of one act. The counselee, student, or worshiper may sometimes feed back his messages by spoken responses or questions.
He also gives many nonverbal responses: facial expressions,
movements, the direction of his gaze. These responses are made
directly to the minister who sent the message but, as the dashed
feedback lines suggest, they respond indirectly to sources—
Biblical, theological, and diagnostic—on which the minister is
presumed to have drawn. In the light of the feedback, it is important that the minister look again at his sources and continue
to draw freshly and more deeply upon them. Thus the feedback
not only influences his adjustment to the receiver and to the

transmission situation but helps him in his own growing understanding and interpretation of his basic sources.

Figure 6. Multichannel Feedback

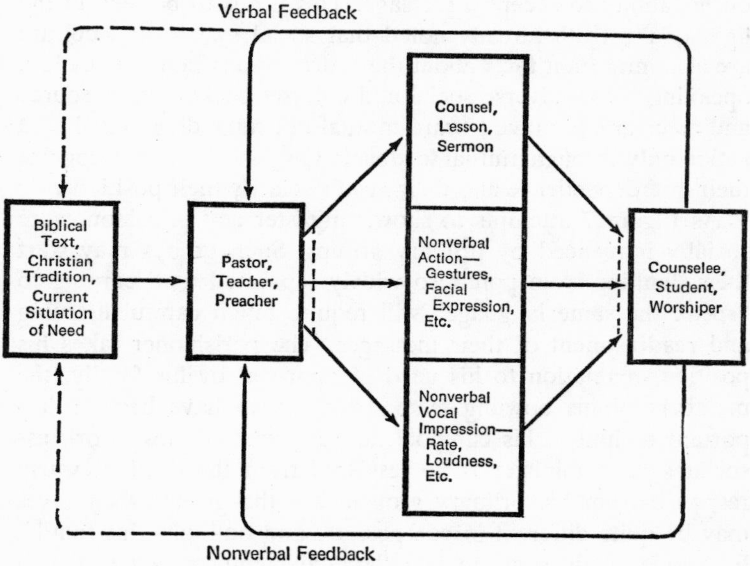

This role of feedback in guiding mutual growth of both
sender and receiver makes it far more than a device by which
the sender finds the sensitive points to which to direct his appeals. For the communicator who enters the interdependent
relation of true communication and is fully sensitive to those
with whom he is dealing, this aspect of feedback makes it a
channel for the reconciliation of differences. Through it a sense
of community can develop. By its aid the parties to the communication can mature together.

Feedback and Social-Cultural Differences

Figure 4 highlighted the relation of the receiver to primary groups and an embracing culture. These have profound effects on his ability to accept a message. This needs to be seen in the light of the truth already noted that social system and culture are also important facts about the source of any communication. Speaking out of diverse social and cultural backgrounds, source and receiver can move toward mutual understanding and shared action only through mutual feedback. Only so can they recognize their interdependence and their need to clarify their positions.

As Figure 7 attempts to show,[6] minister and parishioner are socially influenced by primary groups. Such groups may start their thinking from points so widely separated that learning to "speak the same language" will require much careful listening and readjustment of their messages. The parishioner takes his position in relation to his need of approval by his family, the members of his bowling team, friends who have become important to him in his car pool, and a group of close work associates. The minister is no less free from the need of warm response from his primary groups, but the groups themselves may be quite different in composition and outlook—his family, his service club, a group of influential members of his church board, and a select company of fellow ministers with whom he shares some study and whose approval is important to him. The ways in which these two sets of primary groups think and talk, and the standards by which they measure social responsibility, may be in severe tension with one another. This will require much clarification and adjustment to achieve real communication, even when minister and parishioner are both happily a part of the same culture. If, as the dashed lines in Figure 7 suggest, minister and parishioner belong to different cultures or subcultures, their need for mutual openness and sensitive listening will be multiplied.

Response from another is not effective feedback until it has

Figure 7. Divergent Primary Groups and Cultures

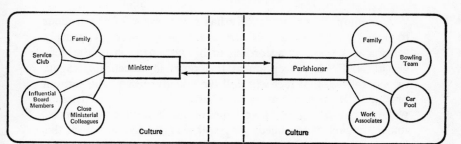

been read and interpreted. The smile on a listener's face may be intended as encouragement, showing that he likes the way things are going and that you have his vote to continue as you are. Or, it may be a polite cover for boredom and the hope that you will get on fairly soon to some other aspect of your subject. Applause at the end of an address may mean hearty approval of what has been said or a conventional ritual marking the end of the exercise. The listener's rapt gaze may indicate fascinated absorption in the presentation, or the maintenance of the decorum of the occasion though the mind is far away. Some aids to interpretation of the meaning of the cues can be found in refined methods of audience analysis; other skills involved in reading feedback grow out of learning to be sensitive not so much to isolated responses as to the total context of the occasion; an important secret of this aspect of communication lies in that art of placing oneself in another's role which we call empathy.

Empathy Leads to Interaction

One practical definition points to empathy as "the process through which we arrive at expectations, anticipations of the internal psychological states of man." [7] This puts the term within the context of role expectations, which we can learn to understand.

A communicator necessarily has some image of the listener to whom he will direct his message. The minister preparing a sermon will shape it according to his visualization of the congregation. If his perception at this point is inaccurate, vague, or generalized, that fact will dull the effectiveness of the sermon produced. If his expectation can sharply define who the listeners will be, something of their state of mind, and some precise understanding of the needs they will bring to the situation, this imaginative taking of their roles will help him to prepare a sermon that can speak usefully to their inner being. In similar fashion, the listener's expectation concerning the speaker—his credibility, good will, knowledge of his subject, and the like— exerts a profound influence on his capacity to respond favorably to what is said.

This mutual taking of the other's role holds an important key to good communication. It is in part a projection of our self-knowledge. From our understanding of ourselves, we draw inferences as to how others feel and think in like circumstances. The more accurate our self-knowledge and the more sympathetic our concerned projection of ourselves into others' situations, the more useful our expectations concerning them may be. Beyond this projected self-knowledge, empathy rests also upon one's imaginatively taking the other's role, feeling one's way into what the other is doing, thinking, feeling. This mutual exchange of roles opens the way to effective interaction in communication. As Berlo puts it, "If two individuals make inferences about their own roles and take the role of the other at the same time, and if their communication behavior depends on the reciprocal taking of roles, then they are communicating by interacting with each other." [8]

Such interaction is the objective of communication in ministry. This chapter has examined seven levels of communication, beginning with the most superficial, transmission, and proceeding in ascending order of significance through contact, feedback, comprehension, acceptance, and internalization, to the goal of interaction. In this chain we have seen feedback as the vital link and have noted that, in itself, response is not feedback; for feedback becomes real only as response is interpreted.

To these matters we shall have numerous occasions to return. Interaction and the reading of feedback are key elements in communicative practice, to be studied in Part Two of this book; and the drawing of useful expectations about communication partners, through accurate inference from our own experience and concerned imagination in taking the other's role, will be central to our thinking in Chapter 4, as we study the analysis of the receiver-interactant.

PROBES

1. For helpful supplementary treatments of the matters discussed in this chapter, see: David K. Berlo, *The Process of Communication: An Introduction to Theory and Practice* (Holt, Rinehart & Winston, Inc., 1960), Ch. 5; Theodore Clevenger and Jack Matthews, *The Speech Communication Process* (Scott, Foresman & Company, 1971), Ch. 8; and Clyde Reid, *The Empty Pulpit: A Study in Preaching as Communication* (Harper & Row, Publishers, Inc., 1967), Ch. 4.

2. Write a brief analysis of the influence of primary groups on your acceptance or rejection of a message or messages relating to some decision you were called upon to make. What primary groups were involved? Were they in agreement in the direction of their influence? What processes of thought and feeling did you go through? How did you finally resolve the conflict? What light, if any, does this throw on your attempts to direct influential messages to others?

3. For one day take special note of how feedback enters into your experience: in classes or other meetings, in informal conversations, in business contacts. Observe the forms feedback takes, in as much detail as you can. In verbal feedback, what was said? In nonverbal feedback, exactly what were the cues?

Was there possibility of more than one interpretation of the responses made? Did you sometimes discover that you had misread a response? What part did your reading of feedback play in your successes and failures as a communicator?

CHAPTER 4

Analyzing the
Receiver-Interactant

Speech communication research has produced valuable studies in "audience analysis." Communicative ministry, however, is concerned not so much with a mass audience as with individual persons. The receiver-interactant may be a member of one's family, a colleague on an administrative board or committee, the intended reader of a letter or news release, or a member of a worshiping congregation. Each of these, in the uniqueness of his own being, with his likeness to and differences from others, is an important communication partner. Skilled communication gains much of its power from ability to anticipate the interactant's meanings and to transmit messages from which intended meanings will arise. In this chapter we study some of the processes that contribute to skill in such analysis.

To analyze another person may, or may not, violate the dialogical relation. Cold examination of another as an object of curiosity or as a target for communication in which one endeavors to manipulate another's responses, denies him personhood. Such analysis makes the other an It, thus interfering with true dialogue. Given concern for the other as a person, however, careful analysis can be incorporated into the relationship, and can contribute to it. A father who loves his son can make his love more useful by careful study of the boy's level of knowledge, the images he shares with his circle of friends, his spontaneous interests, and the probable responses inherent in these and other factors. Such analysis is part of the father's concern, and it helps the father to interact with the boy in dialogue that nurtures growth in both father and son.

Within the dialogical relation the communicative minister can probe questions that help him to make more accurate predictions about the receiver-interactant and so contribute to more significant communication with him.

What Is the Knowledge Level?

The minister can ask, first, What is the level of the receiver's knowledge? There is an almost self-evident need to know something about the other's working vocabulary in order, as far as possible, to reduce the barrier of differing word usage. Too many words not understood, or improperly understood, will garble the message; the receiver may even tire of the effort and "turn us off." On the other hand, a vocabulary that is too elementary may seem patronizing and color the response with resentment toward what seems to insult the listener's intelligence.

Understanding the level of general knowledge will enable the communicator to estimate which facts are needed in a presentation and which can safely be taken for granted. It will guide him in determining how much explanation is needed and what level of complexity may be appropriate. If he is dealing with a group of adult leaders, this level may be quite radically different from the one required by a general congregation with a wide mixture of age groups and educational backgrounds. In the latter instance, the skilled communicator must learn the art of deft simplification and concreteness, which can reach the less advanced yet which moves forward at a pace the better trained can respect.

Beyond the need to understand the general knowledge level lies the question of the receiver's grasp of the special subject matter under discussion. Theodore Clevenger[1] suggests a series of questions designed to serve this purpose:

First, "Does the audience know a problem exists?" It is useless to offer solutions to those who see no problem. In many
instances, Clevenger suggests, a speech may need to utilize a
"problem-solution" design: roughly half the time is used to lay
out the problem and the remaining time is used in suggesting
how it may be handled. For the preacher, the preliminary analysis may reveal that the people addressed are aware of a problem
but that the questions they are asking are in a penultimate form.
The sermon design may then need to be so devised as to begin
with the problem as the listeners now see it, show its relation
to a more ultimate question, and throw the light of the gospel
upon that. For example, the question "How can I find happi-
ness?" is penultimate but may be important to the people addressed. Before the preacher can deal adequately with it, however, he must relate it to the more ultimate question, "How can
I lose myself in something which will command my best and
lead to fulfillment?"

Clevenger's second question, closely related to the strategy
just described, is as follows: "How has the audience formulated
the problem?" People aware of a problem sometimes state it in
a way that skews the possible answers. In civil rights matters,
Clevenger notes, the outcome of consideration will depend on
whether people are saying, "We must pacify these people," or
"We must find some way to meet the needs of these protesting
groups," or "We must find some way to get these agitators out
of the streets," or "We must find more effective means of controlling these outbursts," or "We must find some way of showing
these people the futility of their actions." [2] If a speaker finds
the problem formulated in ways that lead inevitably to wrong
answers, he can do nothing with it until he has helped his
listeners to see a more adequate way of defining it. In many
instances, a message that achieves a more adequate discern-
ment of how to define a problem may be all that one can hope
to accomplish on any given occasion.

Clevenger's third and fourth questions are: "How much information does the audience have?" "Has the auditor considered alternate courses of action?" People often make up their

minds on a subject and then accumulate information in support
of a predetermined decision. In this case they are entrenched
in a feeling of secure knowledge of the subject without having
weighed the available alternatives. In such instances a real
meeting of minds with those who propose courses of action
other than the one to which they are committed becomes doubly
difficult. If this is the case concerning a planned communication,
one needs to be aware of the odds to be faced.

A fifth question inquires, "What criteria will the audience
apply?" Clevenger cites as an example the mutually opposed
criteria of liberal and conservative leaders. On both sides there
is awareness of problems, abundant information, and often a
recognition of similar types of solutions. On one side, however,
there is a commitment to programs broadly undertaken at the
highest levels of government, and on the other there is an insistence that this is unacceptable and that the solutions must
be implemented on a smaller scale, as near to the individual as
possible. To argue other aspects of the problems to be faced
is fruitless unless one takes into account this difference in basic
criteria and deals with it.

Clevenger asks, finally, "Has the audience committed itself
on the question?" Changing a commitment already made entails
grave difficulties and raises serious questions as to whether the
issue at stake justifies the deflection of energy from other weighty
matters that may be involved. In the case of the uncommitted,
one needs to know whether their neutrality is based on a lack of
awareness of the problem, or a feeling that both proposed solutions are so desirable as to make it hard to choose between them,
or a conclusion that both proposals are so undesirable that one
is loath to accept either. In all three cases one is dealing with
the uncommitted, but in each instance the approach to commitment must be different.

While agencies dealing with a wider public may need to use
sophisticated testing devices to determine the answers to such
questions as these, communication in ministry will generally be
well served by information gained by the minister's trained,

sensitive observation. The minister will carefully note the groups to which his people belong and the attitudes that characterize these groups. In his parish calling he will observe what books and periodicals are in use in the homes of his people, learning much about their minds by their reading tastes and habits. He will listen carefully to the attitudes expressed in their conversations, both serious and casual. He will be alert to their radio and television program choices and, in his own viewing of these programs, he will seek to understand not only what the producers are *saying* but what knowledge and attitude levels they are appealing to in their audience.

What Images Operate?

Beyond the question, What is the level of the receiver's knowledge? the minister may ask, What images are operative for those with whom I need to interact? By "image" is meant the associations an object or idea gathers about itself for any individual and the organization of these associations in consciousness. For some people, for instance, the word "Jew" brings to mind certain facial features, unpleasantly pushy social behavior, sharp business practices, and participation in some vague international conspiracy. It is associated with the scribes and Pharisees in the Gospels, with Shylock in Shakespeare, and with the crucifixion of Jesus. This image will seriously affect the one who entertains it, both in his social conduct and in his understanding of the Christian faith. Such an image will color the reception of messages, but it is also true that messages can affect the image.

Several characteristics of people's operative images are worthy of study. For one thing, the communicator needs to know the degree of clarity possessed by any given image. To pursue the illustration of the image of the Jew, it often happens that one who holds such an image maintains it by accommodating within it contradictions that make the picture far from clear. S. I. Hayakawa, discussing prejudice against a hypothetical Mr. Miller, writes: "If Mr. Miller is strange or foreign in his habits, that 'proves' that 'Jews don't assimilate.' If he is thoroughly American—i.e., indistinguishable from other natives—he is 'trying to pass himself off as one of us.' If Mr. Miller fails to give to charity, that is because 'Jews are tight'; if he gives generously, he is 'trying to buy his way into society.' If Mr. Miller lives in the Jewish section of town, that is because 'Jews are so clannish'; if he moves to a locality where there are no other Jews, that is because 'they try to horn in everywhere.' " [3] While the emotional tenacity of this image is strong, its clarity is blurred by contradictory elements whose tensions it cannot resolve. We need to know the clarity of the images that serve as barriers to our message as well as of the images we wish to employ in conveying our meaning.

We also need to know the salience of any given image. How easily is it triggered? How frequently does it come to mind? How likely are other, quite different matters to awaken this image? In the case of the image of the Jew, does it come to mind only occasionally, perhaps at the mention of the word itself, or of a synagogue or a rabbi; or do references to banking, communication, communists, the United Nations, and a host of other subjects associate themselves with it? This factor of salience may suggest a way of communicating with persons whose images are so firmly fixed as to be immune to direct attack: we may begin to build new "triggering" associations. To one who holds the negative image of the Jew it can be emphasized, from time to time, that Jesus was a Jew, Paul was a Jew, the prophets were Jews, God used Jews to write most of the Biblical documents, and it was a Jewish prophet who wrote in a Jewish book still important to Judaism the highest ethical conception of religious obligation: "What does the LORD require of you but to do justice, and to love kindness, and to walk humbly with your God?" (Micah 6:8). Invulnerable to open debate, the image gains a changed quality of salience as new associations are carefully and patiently built around it.

We need, concerning any image, to know not only its clarity and salience but also its coherence. How consistent are its own parts with one another? How well does it hang together in a unified whole? Here again there may be a suggestion of a possible means of communication: while one cannot disturb the image by frontal assault, it may be possible to introduce dissonance within it. One can share his own respect for a Jewish friend who, at great cost to himself, kept his plant running through a long depression—when it would have been to his economic advantage to close down—because of his sense of loyalty to his employees and obligation to his community, many of whose people would have been thrown out of work in the repercussions of the closing. One can introduce Jewish friends of culture and refinement. One can provide occasions of dialogue with rabbis who, without losing any of their commitment to Judaism, know and love the New Testament, respect Jesus, and can teach us elements of an understanding of him that we had previously missed. Thus, without debating the seemingly unshakable image, one can introduce dissonant elements that call for accommodation and thus ultimately change meanings.

We need, further, to know the integration of a receiver's images. Are they related to other images to produce an organized body of thought? To the degree that communication can help the receiver to relate healthy images to each other organically, it ministers to growth and personal wholeness. Learning to know the clarity, salience, coherence, and integration of the images held by those with whom we communicate is thus a vital factor in our ability to help them.

Making Pastoral Analysis

In his analysis of the receiver-interactant, the minister can consider what analytic methods are peculiarly open to him as a minister. Some methods are integral to the pastoral office and its own distinctive traditions. Intercessory prayer is an example. It would be false to advocate prayer for others as a device for knowing them better; to pray for them for reasons other than one's concern for their need is to take a decisive step toward undermining prayer altogether. But it is also true that concerned prayer for others so teaches one to put himself in another's place that it deepens insight into the other's life. The pastor who methodically lifts up a few names from his membership roll in day-by-day intercession deepens his empathic understanding while he prays.

Closely allied with this discipline is the minister's weekly inventory of freshly perceived needs among his people. As an early step in the preparation of a sermon, the minister can write on his worksheet the initials of a dozen or more of his people with whom he has had some significant pastoral contact in the preceding week. These persons come especially to mind in this context because of needs he has sensed in them. Opposite each set of initials he writes a brief sentence stating the need: a problem one finds overwhelming, a temptation with which another struggles, a decision still another must make; here a grief to be worked through, there a guilt to be dealt with, a suffering to be borne, a conflict to be managed, a success to be assimilated, a drudging task to be seen through to the end, a new love to be hallowed, or a betrayed love whose wound will not heal. What he writes down are not abstractions about the human condition; they are names or initials linked with vivid faces and poignant scenes that reveal tangible present reality.

The sermon he must now prepare is not a general discussion of some theme, to be addressed to a generalized entity called a congregation. It is a part of a continuing dialogue with these very specific individual persons. Seeing their faces, recalling the conversations that opened their needs to his pastoral view, picturing the scenes in which these needs became apparent, he has a matchless means of audience analysis. Here is a living cross section of next Sunday's congregation.

In thus visualizing his people, the minister will respect the confidential character of his relationship with them. Of course he will not describe incidents and situations others might recognize! But in the further steps in preparation of his sermon he will be aware of these persons and their needs. All that he does will be a part of a conversation in which he brings from the gospel whatever light he can to guide their way. As he speaks out of vivid knowledge of this week's handful of persons, freshly visualized and empathically understood, many others of whom he is not aware, but whose needs are not dissimilar, will find his meanings meeting theirs in ways that minister to their need.

Employing Published Materials

A part of the minister's reading can help him diagnose the needs of his congregation. A body of useful literature has been produced as able writers, listening widely to all kinds of people, have reported what they heard. Bill Moyers' *Listening to America* belongs to such literature. "In Washington," he wrote, "I helped to draft legislation which we hoped would make this a better country. In New York I belonged to a profession whose express purpose is to communicate with people. But I learned that it is possible to write bills and publish newspapers without knowing what the country is about or who the people are. . . . I wanted to hear people speak for themselves." [4] With his tape recorder, Moyers traveled extensively over the country, talking to wide varieties of people about what concerned them, faithfully reporting the conversations. Such a book may not be specific analysis of the immediate persons with whom one deals, but it provides important background that takes one into the lives of a multitude of people and supplies material out of which local insights may be sharpened.

John Steinbeck's *Travels with Charley* is another example of this literature. Steinbeck discovered that, living in the East for twenty-five years, he was writing about life in an America he could reconstruct only from memory. "And the memory," he said, "is at best a faulty, warpy reservoir. . . . I knew the changes only from books and newspapers. . . . So it was that I determined to look again, to try to rediscover this monster land. Otherwise, in writing, I could not tell the small diagnostic truths which are the foundations of the larger truth." [5] In his camper truck, largely incognito, Steinbeck covered the continent, visiting with people in tourist camps, wayside drive-ins, and a host of other such places, his perceptive ear attuned to the speech and mind of his countrymen, bringing back his own vivid report.

These books are cited only to make concrete the literary genre implied. The value of such writing, generally speaking, lies in its currency; but there is a continuing production of such books, and some familiarity with them can sharpen the minister's perception of the minds he encounters, even while it provides him with wider understanding of the currents of his time to which his own people are responding.

Discerning Contemporary Axioms

In gathering background on the people and the times, the minister need not rely totally on skilled reporting by others. He can make his own ventures in deriving what may be called the axioms of his contemporaries. The newspapers and magazines of widest circulation in his community provide a means to such study. Every periodical has what has been termed its own "personality"—that mix of characteristics, style, interests, and assumptions about its readers which attracts its following. Assumptions about the readers focus the study of axioms. The mix differs from one journal to another as these assumptions vary. The journal's ability to attract mass readership in a competitive market provides some claim to objective validation of its assumptions. For this reason there are two quite divergent ways for a communicator to read periodicals.

In addition to reading them for information and entertainment, one can read in search of their unspoken assumptions about their readers. What in their reader, as they perceive him, makes them play up one set of items rather than another? What does the array of feature items tell about the reader's images? What does the writing style indicate concerning the knowledge level assumed? What do the advertising appeals reveal concerning the motivations on which advertisers are willing—with much show of success—to bet large numbers of advertising dollars? When one has studied an issue, or a series of issues, of a journal widely followed among his people, he can distill his impressions into brief axiomatic statements. If he has done his work well, he can rest some cautious confidence in these axioms as more or less valid pointers to the things these readers take for granted, probably never fully articulating them even to themselves. Such axioms can claim no specific accuracy about any given individual, but in conjunction with other indicators they tell much that will help the communicative minister to make accurate predictions about the meanings with which his message must interact.[6]

A Pastoral Overview

More specific methods of evoking feedback to keep analysis up to date await attention in Chapter 6. In the present discussion, we have seen some ways of evaluating the receiver's knowledge level, noting that his awareness of whether a problem exists, his formulation of it, his sensitivity to alternative answers, his criteria for decision, and the degree and nature of commitment already present, all indicate needs to be met and methods to be used in the communication. We have seen that images, as well as knowledge, are important to the analysis, and that the clarity, salience, coherence, and integration of the receiver's images help us to understand him, and suggest ways of working with him. Some methods of analysis peculiarly available to the minister have come into view: sensitive observation in pastoral visiting and other contacts, that sharpened awareness of persons which is nurtured by intercessory prayer, the pinpointing of the needs of individuals in a weekly pastoral inventory, rounding out personal perceptions through the reading of literature that undertakes skillful diagnosis of the current mind, and the deriving of axioms that may be useful indicators of the knowledge and images operative among one's people.

These methods must be employed, not in cold treatment of

others as specimens for study, but in implementing personal concern. So used, supported constantly by the effort empathically to put oneself in the other's role, they can be invaluable aids to a communicative ministry.

PROBES

1. Further treatment of the concerns of this chapter will be found in Theodore Clevenger, *Audience Analysis* (The Bobbs-Merrill Company, Inc., 1966), and in Merrill R. Abbey, *Preaching to the Contemporary Mind* (Abingdon Press, 1963). Both books take receiver analysis as a central problem, the first from a stance within the field of public address, the second from the more specialized viewpoint of homiletics.

2. In this chapter, the study of images has been illustrated by reference to an unfortunate stereotype of the Jew. From careful observation of some group (a class, a small congregation, a well-known neighborhood) make your own analysis of the image that the group holds of Negroes, Mexicans, the National Council of Churches, or some other identifiable group or organization. As far as possible, utilize the categories of clarity, salience, coherence, and integration as analytic tools.

3. Make further analysis of the selected group, with special regard to their relation to some problem or proposition of current concern, using as your analytic method the application of Clevenger's six questions listed under the subhead, "What Is the Knowledge Level?"

4. From a study of an issue of a periodical widely read among members of the selected group (surveying editorial content and/or advertising appeals), distill a set of "contemporary axioms" based on the assumptions the journal seems to be making about its readers.

CHAPTER 5

Learning
the Language of Media

The electric media have created a new communications world. Their effect is not confined to messages they convey or methods they use; these media plunge us into a completely altered environment. "The sheer quantity of information conveyed by press-magazine-film-TV-radio far exceeds the quantity of information conveyed by school instruction and texts." [1] This generalization by Marshall McLuhan is mathematically true. Surveys reveal that the average eighteen-year-old youth has watched 15,000 hours of television and seen 500 feature-length motion pictures—has spent nearly 16,000 hours with these two media alone. But from kindergarten through high school he has had only 10,800 hours of formal instruction. Such data support the McLuhan conclusion that "the new media are not ways of relating us to the old 'real' world; they are the real world and they reshape what remains of the old world at will." [2]

It is this reshaping which gives rise to McLuhan's aphorism, "The medium is the message." This does not mean that, so long as we use the right media, messages are no longer important. Messages remain so valuable that dollar-motivated advertisers often spend more on filming a one-minute commercial than on the program that attracts the audience. The medium is the message in the sense that the very existence of a new medium reconstructs the environment. The electric light changes the relation of night and day: in 1971, for instance, World Series baseball—once strictly a daytime event—began to be played at night. Electricity alters the relation of indoors and outdoors: reading, crafts, and evening games once confined to the living room now move to the park or patio; baseball comes indoors at the Astrodome. Another medium, the automobile, creates superhighways; transforms the shape of cities; revolutionizes many aspects of the economy; and, in a half hour's drive, provides a new anonymity that profoundly alters the moral environment. Media are themselves messages that reconstruct our living space and our life-style.

Media not only are messages; they also carry messages. Carrying messages in new ways, media influence the habits of perception developed by their audience. Conditioned by film and television, people alter their reception of all messages. The youth who has viewed 16,000 hours of electric media programming does not bring to the classroom or church service the same kind of mind as did his counterpart of an earlier generation. A communicative ministry, in order to reach him, must learn the perceptual language that the new media have evolved. For electric media erect new barriers to communication even as they bestow new aids in winging the message.

Although a single chapter cannot presume to teach the language of media, it can point out some directions for further reflection and study. What we essay in this chapter is not the task, necessarily specialized, of guiding skills in broadcasting or other media activities. Rather, we seek light on the question: How does the new world of media influence our total communicative task?

Understanding Media-conditioned Minds

Communicators need awareness of the profound ways in which the new media condition all receivers. This is apparent in what McLuhan calls the laying bare of the contemporary individual's central nervous system. Every medium, he observes, is an extension of man. The wheel extends our foot, increasing our range and rate of travel. The bow and arrow, the gun or missile, extends the fist. The microphone extends the voice.

With every extension of man there is, in McLuhan's term, an "autoamputation." The automobile, which extends my feet, in a sense "amputates" them; my feet are not as available for use as were my grandfather's when he walked what is for me an impossible distance in opening a new western frontier. The microphone has so "amputated" our vocal organs that, whereas speakers of another day profoundly moved outdoor audiences running into thousands, we need a public-address system in the nave of a small church. The "autoamputation" that is inherent in our extensions, McLuhan notes, could not be endured except by numbing.

In the case of the electric media, it is the central nervous system that is extended. Our sensitive receptors and their apparatus of perception are now laid bare. They are bombarded by impressions that converge with a total all-at-onceness from all parts of the world, day and night. We rise and retire to the accompaniment of news broadcasts and hear them in the interludes of travel that, until our time, exposed people to new scenes but isolated them from such news communication. At such times as New Year's Day many of us are "present" not at one football game but at a parade of Bowl games from many parts of the country. Scenes of war, riot, and assassination are no longer reported in extra editions of newspapers; they are directly experienced. In the all-at-onceness of the electric media our nervous systems are exposed. We can endure the pain only by a numbing process that produces the phenomenon of quick excitement and quick forgetfulness that easily becomes apathy.

Yet we are "involved" by these media. The "involvement" of the McLuhan age, however, does not refer to the empathic entrance into the situation of another that this same term has often connoted. The "involvement" of which McLuhan makes us aware is a property of what he calls "cool" media. A medium is termed "hot" or "cool" according to the sharpness of definition of the image it projects. Radio is confined to sound, but it delivers the sound image with high definition, and is thus a "hot" medium. Television, giving both picture and sound, presents an image less sharply defined than the one projected on the cinema screen. The television picture is the product of swiftly moving light particles on lines produced by the tube. It is made into a picture for us only as eye and perceiving mind create the wholes. There are no "frames" as in the successive exposures of the motion picture; at any given moment we must create the "frames" from the lights and shadows moving across the screen. This low-definition, "cool" medium involves us in the process, requiring more of us than "hot" media do.

As a "cool" medium, television develops an expectation that we will be thus involved in completing a communication. A telecast of a symphony orchestra supplies an example. In a concert hall, music lovers sit enthralled with the beautiful sound and the relatively unchanging visual image. When an orchestra comes to the television tube, however, the music is only an accompanying part of the visual image created by the roving camera. The camera highlights first one section and then another, plays up and down the rows of brass or strings, or strives for startling effects and intriguing angles. It is television's nature to involve us in putting the orchestra together out of such pieces as it supplies. As a matter of fact, a symphony concert, thus rendered a less clearly defined sound experience, changed into a low-definition visual-with-sound, is not very good television. A symphony rehearsal, on the other hand, can be a fascinating television show precisely because it presents something unfinished, in process of being put together. It involves us in the struggle for completion.

Conditioned by our habits of such involvement with cool media, we are exposed to war, disaster, and violence of all kinds as they come into our living rooms. We are "involved," not so much with the people trapped in these situations as with the moving images. War's filth does not litter the living room or make a shambles of the house. We witness a murder, but there is no blood on our carpet. Faces are distorted with unbearable pain, but after a thirty-second segment the picture is replaced by another scene. We are not involved with persons who make demands on us. In the passing show, there is little time for real empathy. We talk of being "involved," but our real exchange is with the phenomena of the medium. The demands of humane concern are not absent, but they drop into a relatively secondary place.

Whatever his medium, the communicator deals with persons whose responses are conditioned by these effects of the baring of the central nervous system. Of three results, present in every receiver, the skilled communicator must be aware: (*a*) He lives immersed in all-at-onceness and comes to any communication already full of impressions, frustrations, and information (which may be misinformation because it seems complete despite its fragmentation). (*b*) He survives the experience only because he is largely numbed, and the apathy thus produced may become a social and spiritual problem. (*c*) He knows best how to deal with communications that come to him in a "cool" form (a form that involves him in the completion of the message). These effects call for long and concerned study and adaptation by the minister-communicator.

All-at-onceness and Exposure in Depth

Two other characteristics of the media-conditioned receiver should be noted. Although McLuhan may have overstressed the first—the movement from linear to simultaneous perception—its importance must not be overlooked. In the age of the written and printed word, the linear mode was all-important. One by one, letters were put together into words, which were strung into sentences, which in turn were arranged in paragraphs; and these were ordered in point-by-point development of marshaled argument, which moved in a straight line to a conclusion. With the electric media all is different. Impressions come from everywhere with little order among them. Not only is the montage a favored art form for these media; the media make of each day's experience a montage of impressions.

The effect of this conditioning is multiple:

1. Although the mind must still begin somewhere and proceed along orderly lines to a conclusion, we are growing less patient with the point-by-point development of an idea. Presentation may have to begin "where the action is"—the most moving part of the story or the outcome of the process—and move back to pick up parts of the rationale or background as they become relevant.

2. Minds more accustomed to the simultaneous than the linear are conditioned to a "total nowness" that suggests something significant about style in any presentation. The style most congruent with media habits of mind is not the discursive unfolding of story line or argument, but the plunge into a situation that source and receiver then seek to put together, the receiver being left with his considerable share of the process to complete for himself.

3. Minds thus conditioned are no longer content with the role of the distant spectator; they expect to be drawn into the communication. McLuhan reports that medical students sense less immediacy in watching actual surgery in the operating theater than in seeing the same operation projected from a closeup camera on closed circuit television. In the latter, they have a sense of participation that they lack in the former. If ministry seeks to cultivate what Paul Tillich called "ultimate concern," this need of the media-conditioned mind calls for careful attention.

The other effect of this conditioning has to do with what McLuhan calls exposure "in depth." Stereo, with its "wraparound sound," which completely engulfs the listener, is one of the experiences of depth to which he refers. Television, gripping us by both sound and sight and involving us in the completion of its "cool," low-definition picture, is another. It is to be noted that depth, in this sense, refers not to the profundity of the subject or its treatment, but to these aspects of sense perception. For this reason, McLuhan's next statement is startling: "Anything approached in depth acquires as much interest as the greatest matters. Because 'depth' means 'in inter-relation,' not in isolation." [3]

This, in its turn, has its own multiple implications:

1. Experiences carry the greatest interest when we are deeply immersed in them; multiple media may be a case in point. "Insight," McLuhan observes, "is a kind of mental involvement in process" [4]—which may suggest that the most useful communicative ministry emerges from situations that draw the receiver into full participation.

2. In a world of electric media the church's word and act become parts of one total "wrap-around" message. Having brought the microphone and the television camera into the sanctuary, we must not delude ourselves that they will report only the messages we select. Mercilessly they report a total situation and, to the degree that receivers are interested, it is that total situation which involves them. If there is dissonance between word and act, it is—more than ever—fatal.

3. Interrelation is essential to witness. Minds accustomed to "mental involvement in process" are not content merely to listen to what we say. To reach them, it is necessary to involve them: to listen to them, to ask questions as well as make statements, to value what they say, and to expose ourselves to the total risk of an encounter that cannot be fully preplanned and controlled.

Getting Involved with Open Communication

A communicative ministry has need for involvement, not only with media-conditioned minds, but with the media themselves. Ministry that serves the world as well as the church implies concerned stewardship of media that, for good or ill, change the world. It is not enough to learn how to *use* media; Christian caring involves a concern for their development in a manner that brings out their full potential.

William Fore points out one aspect of such concern as he
distinguishes between "open" and "closed" communication.
Mass media, he says, can open man's world "by extending his
eyes and ears to take in a wide range of information not otherwise available." But, he adds, they can also close man's world,
making the receiver "less, rather than more, of a person. The
cliché analysis, the formula drama, the ten-second 'news' report, the repetitious and insulting advertising claim, the mis-
leading headline, the emotional picture and the sensationalized
report—all these tend to cut man off from reality rather than
to relate him to it." [5]

There is much to indicate that the broadcast media have
come nearer to a diet of "closed" communication than to the
achievement of their potential for "opening" the world. At the
end of a week of around-the-clock monitoring of New York
City's five principal television channels, Charles Sopkin concluded: "I naïvely expected that the ratio would run three to
one in favor of trash. It turned out to be closer to a hundred
to one." [6] This judgment is confirmed by numerous studies of
the implications of television as more fully an advertising than
a communications enterprise.

Developments in public broadcasting, educational television,
and some notable programs carried on the commercial channels,
demonstrate the vast potential of this medium for open communication. It is part of Christian stewardship to share in the
endeavor to help concerned people in this medium to realize
its amazing potential as a true "extension" of man rather than
a blocking and closing in of his life.

The Mixed Media Presentation

Media involvement further implies the learning of the uses
of the multimedia campaign and the mixed media presentation.
Our familiar term "multimedia" is generally stretched to cover
both of these, but two quite separate processes are involved.
By "mixed media presentation" we mean a presentation that

combines in one experience the use of such varied media as slides, motion picture film, a recorded sound track, and the like. It combines the advantages of involvement in depth, already discussed, with those of redundancy; that is, providing more information, in more ways, than is strictly necessary to the statement of an idea or message, and thus providing added insurance against information loss in the transmission. Redundancy is an important part of all communication, exemplified in the statement, restatement, and illustration used in all good writing and speaking. The mixed media presentation gives redundancy an added dimension by rounding out the message on simultaneous multiple channels. Its uses are varied:

1. Mixed media may be used to stimulate useful discussion. For instance, a sound track of recorded music with, perhaps, occasional spoken script, may accompany slide projections on several screens, throwing variant definitions of such a word as "discipline" into juxtaposition with scenes from contemporary life that either reinforce or challenge the ideas. Following such a presentation, lively and productive group sharing may ensue.

2. Mixed media may be used for vivid explanation of an otherwise abstract concept, as in the case of an explanatory lecture, with possible recorded music or taped voice inserts, accompanied by illustrative slides or film on one or more screens.

3. Mixed media may round out an experience in multilayered form. In one such experience the sound track was provided by the rock opera records of *Jesus Christ Superstar,* and the visual presentation utilized three screens. On one screen the libretto of the production was projected, to help the audience follow the words of the fast-moving songs. The other two screens carried appropriate scenes from the life of Jesus, taken from classic and modern sources, in juxtaposition with contemporary news scenes that provided parallels, contrasts, or startling commentary. Numerous other uses, to provide redundant clarity of explanation, or "in depth" involvement in process, can be devised.

The Multimedia Campaign

In the multimedia campaign, various media are employed, one by one, in cumulative impact over a period of time, to achieve one sharply defined objective. Stanley J. Rowland, Jr., writing in 1968, suggested, as an example, how a multimedia campaign could be used by the churches toward peace in Vietnam. He showed how, using such an approach, the churches could put powerfully before the country the peace objectives most denominations had enunciated.[7] As he lays out the steps, they would begin with a definition of the problem: How to involve the masses in knowledge of the situation, leading to action for peace? With personal involvement as a goal, they might then determine to use involving media—television, radio, film, and recorded sound.

A survey of available channels might reveal such open possibilities as the already preempted Sunday morning radio and television time, perhaps a prime time special or two, the film and slide projectors available to most churches, the abundant numbers of home record players, and the readiness of many church people to "read up" on a subject that excites them.

With these channels in mind, the work of production would begin with the formulation of a unifying concept; in this case, "Viet-Quest." This would be broken down into such parts as "Viet-Quest for information," "Viet-Quest for people-to-people contacts," "Viet-Quest for prisoner exchanges," "Viet-Quest for negotiation."

Such preliminary thinking would then be translated into the language of the media. Graphic artists would be employed to provide visual imagery. The Viet-Quest concept would be basically stated in a ninety-minute film documentary loaded with facts and with little or no direct advocacy. From this would be spun off two thirty-minute television documentaries, which would be aired at the best time obtainable and followed by the fuller ninety-minute film made available for church showings.

A twenty-minute slide show would also be prepared from the same basic source, with a recorded sound track, possibly using additional sound to compensate for the loss of the moving image. So the campaign would go, augmented by a printed booklet for further information, a book of pictures and captions from the original film, a record disc of songs and poetry by soldiers in Vietnam, postcards carrying pictures of the destruction and a prayer for peace, and cassette-recorded interviews with soldiers just returned from the fighting.

Such a case, although hypothetical, suggests the possibilities of the multimedia campaign, which awaits utilization by the church at such time as Christians are ready to make the all-out investment in some major concern.

PROBES

1. Space limitations in the present work have allowed only a suggestive opening sketch of media concerns. These concerns should be pursued through further reading. In this area, Marshall McLuhan's provocative writing is focal; his basic book is *Understanding Media: The Extensions of Man* (McGraw-Hill Book Co., Inc., 1964). Stan Opotowsky, *TV: The Big Picture* (E. P. Dutton & Co., Inc., 1961), presents a nontechnical exposition of all phases of American television up to its date, and Martin Mayer, *About Television* (Harper & Row, Publishers, Inc., 1972), rounds out subsequent developments. Fred W. Friendly, *Due to Circumstances Beyond Our Control* (Random House, Inc., 1967), chronicles the difficulties encountered by the former president of CBS News in his attempts to render responsible stewardship of network documentary facilities. Nicholas Johnson, *How to Talk Back to Your Television Set* (Little, Brown & Company, 1970), contains the reflections of a crusading member of the Federal Communications Commission on how to upgrade television fare. Merrill R. Abbey, *Man, Media, and the Message* (Friendship Press, 1970), Ch. 5, gives a résumé of the church's ventures in the broadcasting field. B. F.

Jackson, Jr., ed., *Television-Radio-Film for Churchmen* (Communication for Churchmen series, Vol. II; Abingdon Press, 1969), is a practical manual of church communication through the broadcast media. William F. Fore, *Image and Impact: How Man Comes Through in the Mass Media* (Friendship Press, 1970), guides the reader to a theological evaluation of current programming.

2. You can take a significant step toward equipping yourself for stewardship of the broadcast media by monitoring a network during the prime time hours for an evening or a series of evenings. This involves thoughtful viewing and careful note-taking. William Fore suggests the questions such monitoring should bear steadily in mind: "Consider what is being *implied* on that screen about the nature of man. With half your mind on the flickering images, use the other half to ask questions such as these:

"Are the men and women *things* or *persons?*

"Are there 'sacred cows' in evidence—*things* and *ideas* that the medium treats as if they were gods?

"Is man so good he becomes unbelievable? or Godlike?

"Does good always win over evil?

"Is man the final good?

"Are there other loyalties more important than life itself?

"Is man's responsibility suggested, or is it avoided?

"Is it lifelike or phony?

"Try reflecting on the commercials, too. . . .

"Try cutting through the mere content to discover the *assumptions*. Often they are nonverbal, noncontent and quite hidden. But they are present in every program, and if you don't find them, you will be the loser." [8]

Is man treated as a mere consumer? Is selling the overriding objective?

How many members of minority groups appear in the programs? in news coverage? in commercials? What image of minority groups is projected? What is the percentage of minority group representatives in proportion to the total number of par-

The log of such a monitoring project will provide important correctives and documentation for your general impressions of the media. Against this informed and thoughtful background further steps toward media stewardship can be taken.

PART TWO

Communicative
Proclamation

CHAPTER 6

Preaching in a Multichannel Milieu

Among communicative ministries—which reach far beyond the pulpit—preaching holds a place of unique importance. The minister's other communications deal chiefly with individuals or small groups; his preaching serves an inclusive cross section of his parish. What he does in this ministry, serving his largest public, goes far to create the spiritual climate in which all his other work with persons will be either advanced or handicapped.

Not every minister will make preaching his speciality, but the image he presents as he preaches will have a determining effect upon any other vocational function in which he hopes to make his influence most profoundly felt. He may think of counseling and the pastoral care of individuals as his field of most useful service. If so, preaching can establish the precounseling relationship. No other professional counseling group has a parallel opportunity to establish a bond with persons before individual counseling begins. One national survey revealed that 42 percent of the population—more than those who responded to any other professional group—said it would be their clergyman to whom they would turn first in times of emotional stress.[1] Whether many members of any given congregation will be among that number will depend, in no small degree, on the understanding, approachableness, and competence that listeners perceive in the minister's preaching. Moreover, once the counseling relation is established, the minister has a priceless opportunity to reinforce his work by the insights he nurtures in his sermons.

If he aspires to an educational ministry, he can be grateful for the opportunity afforded to him as preacher. There is no other public forum in his community for which, week in and week out across the years, so many of the adult population regularly set aside time, leave their homes and other preoccupations, and give thoughtful attention to something said to them on the major issues of life. If the minister fritters away this hearing with hastily assembled "inspirational" messages on a miscellany of topics, that is a judgment upon him rather than upon the potential of the pulpit. In the hands of a thoughtful man who gives diligent study and careful planning to his task, the preaching office can be a major educational enterprise.

Hoping to make his contribution through an administrative ministry that enables the church as fellowship and institution to rise to the full height of its possibilities for service, the minister must take cognizance of the part his preaching will play. In his pulpit he generates the atmosphere in which much of the life of the institution will be lived. By his preaching he can influence the goals and deepen the motives that give vitality to the fellowship and its undertakings. The role or style he establishes in the pulpit—e.g., authoritarian director, charismatic leader, pastoral enabler—will color all his administrative relations with persons.

For ministers who envision the work of social change as their primary contribution, a statement by sociologist Jeffrey K. Hadden is significant: "While they may not presume to speak 'in the name of' or 'for' the church, there can be little doubt that their voice takes on considerable legitimacy because they are the professional leadership of large religious institutions." Because this is true, Hadden points out that the ultimate effectiveness of the minister as change agent will be determined largely by his persuasiveness *within* his congregation: "The more strongly clergy attempt to engage laity, the more solid will be the base of a new, challenge-oriented church." This does not foreclose the possibility of more direct methods, Hadden points out, but it does suggest that the minister's power base is in the consolidation of conviction within his own congregation: "While converting the Christians is perhaps a more difficult task than carrying a picket sign, the long-range results would seem to be more promising for achieving significant social change." [2] A wise preaching ministry can exert profound influence in effecting such conversion within the church.

The Power of the Embodied Word

Even in a multimedia age, the spoken word has power. When words are forged into a message embodied in a convincing *person,* they become a medium as powerful as any that the age of electric media has produced. Persuasive public address, incarnate in the fanaticism of Adolf Hitler, built the Third Reich; and the spoken message to which Winston Churchill had devoted a lifetime of painstaking skill development turned the tide of World War II. Those who discount the continuing power of messages so embodied to move men in a later period must take into account the revolutionary power of the spoken word of Fidel Castro in galvanizing attention and stirring people to action in the Latin world and the power of the sayings of Mao Tse-tung in building a new China. "Preaching," said Phillips Brooks, "is the bringing of truth through personality." [3] Among the powerful media of our time, truth through personality is still a force of primary potency.

Yet the preacher now works in a multichannel milieu, and his pulpit ministry must be related to other media. How well we ask the basic question will determine the adequacy of our understanding of the relation between preaching and other media. To inquire whether preaching is useful in a world of media is to ask a question too vague to be revealing. To ask whether preaching is as nearly adequate a way of delivering the message as other media might be leaves the problem still unfocused. We need rather to analyze the goal that any communication is intended to reach and then to ask, What medium can best achieve *this* goal under *these* circumstances and *with the resources at my disposal?* Careful educators go even further in their field, and subdivide the media question:

"1. What kinds of messages should be transmitted orally in the classroom?
2. What kinds of messages should be transmitted visually, through books?
3. What kinds of messages should be transmitted visually, but nonverbally, through pictures, rather than words?
4. What kinds of messages should be transmitted physically, through touch, by having students actually perform certain tasks, examine and manipulate certain objects, etc.?" [4]

The minister should be no less careful in his assessment of the relationship of preaching to other channels of communication at his command. The remainder of this chapter attempts to deal with factors central to that relationship.

The Spoken Word in Perspective

The minister who would make maximum use of his preaching potential must learn to cope with the limitations of the spoken word. Research has documented the assertion that people tend to listen chiefly to what already has their agreement. For example, persons interviewed four weeks after buying a new automobile indicated that in the preceding week they had read more advertisements of the car they had just purchased than of any other make. Persons who had not made a recent car selection showed no such bias in their reading of advertising.[5] Likewise, in a political campaign, surveys show that most persons listen to more speeches and read more releases by members of their own party than by any of the opposition.[6] This does not mean that political oratory is useless; other research indicates that the political speech serves to deepen the conviction of the faithful, even when it is of limited effectiveness in converting the opposition.[7]

Research indicates, further, that people tend to perceive messages addressed to them in ways that harmonize with values they already hold. "Communications condemning racial discrimination, for example, have been interpreted by prejudiced persons as favoring such discrimination. Persons who smoke cigarettes, to take another example, were found to be . . . much less likely to become convinced that smoking actually caused cancer."[8]

To compound these limitations, research indicates the tendency of most people to avoid messages that seem threatening. Not only do smokers *alter their perception* of messages relating cigarette smoking to the incidence of cancer; it was found that those who smoke were *much less likely to read* or attend to messages dealing with this relation than were nonsmokers.[9]

Since one objective of preaching is to induce change in persons, findings such as these sound a warning note. While they do not support the conclusion that all preaching intended to influence change is futile, *they indicate ways in which preachers can define objectives and employ methods that work within the discovered limitations.* (*a*) Even though preaching alone is not likely to turn many persons from one course of thought or action to another that is diametrically opposed, it can strengthen the commitment of the wavering, and it can empower the faithful for witness and service. (*b*) Although attacks on people's prejudices may not dissolve them, the skillful communicator can introduce elements of dissonance into deeply entrenched positions. This may lead to their ultimate modification. (*c*) While preaching that threatens men may lose its effect because the threat inhibits real hearing, preaching that emphasizes the "good news" of the Christian message, that puts the law always in the context of the gospel, has power to get through this barrier. A distinguished nuclear physicist was asked: "As a scientist, do you have any message for theologians?" The physicist replied: "Tell us what the good news is. At my church I hear frequent exhortation about some good news which Christians are supposed to share with the world. But I hear little about *what it is*. Tell us what the good news *is*." A preaching ministry which responds to that appeal, which puts its demands for change in the constant context of concrete, specific good news, will not be tuned out.

The Opinion-Change Network

Learning to work within the limitations of the spoken word, the minister who would make the most of his preaching opportunity must take a further step: he must recognize and respond to the place of public address within the opinion-change network. We have already noted the power of primary groups to influence or inhibit proposed changes in thought and conduct. Preaching meant to induce change must take such group pressures into account and relate the message to them. It must also be set in the context of pastoral care that works toward more helpful group life. The role of "opinion leaders" in effecting change in any group is highly significant.

For example, extensive research has been devoted to the ways in which new methods come to be adopted by farmers, physicians, and others. Such research has shown that, within a group, identifiable opinion leaders play a decisive part. Public presentations through lectures, farm or professional journals, and the like, are not without effect; but in most cases the actual adoption of the new procedure is brought about by the influence of face-to-face contact with someone locally respected among the farmers or doctors being studied. Generally in one geographical area the same person or small group of persons plays the opinion leader role for all who make the change. This does not mean, however, that the public presentation is unimportant. A study of the opinion leaders reveals that invariably they hear more lectures, attend more meetings, and read more journals than do any of the persons whom they influence.

Furthermore, in addition to its educational value in training the opinion leaders, the public presentation—the lecture or journal material—serves all who adopt the new method. (*a*) It makes them aware that a problem exists, and it stimulates their interest in finding a solution. (*b*) It alerts them to an alternative procedure of which they had not been aware. (*c*) Once the influence of the opinion leader has made the group ready to try the new course of action, such material provides the group with the necessary detailed information concerning the steps to be taken.[10]

It is a reasonable inference from such studies that preaching can take its place in this chain of opinion change. The evidence points to the self-defeat of those who suppose that preaching alone will work the desired transformation. To be discouraged and frustrated by the failure of a sermon or a course of sermons to induce the desired transformation is unnecessary and unwise. Instead of such false hopes or such discouragement, the preacher needs to have a clear view of what his preaching can do in making hearers aware of needs, possible alternatives, and further steps they can take in the nurture of new ways of thought and action, once they are adopted. He needs also to see the value of preaching in training and informing the witness of those who will influence others. He needs, finally, to find and use methods that will maximize the usefulness of preaching in the network of channels leading to change.

The Sermon Seminar

Emerging methods for making preaching integral to a two-way communication, for adapting it to the opinion-change network, take varied forms. One model is that of the *sermon seminar.* The seminar procedure varies only slightly with the size of the congregation. In churches of a relatively small size, the minister meets his group on a Monday night, looking toward the next Sunday, or on a week night, looking toward a Sunday ten days to two weeks removed, to consider with them a sermon in preparation. He opens the session with a brief exegetical study of the Bible passage on which the sermon is to be based. The purpose of this statement is not to indicate a shape for the sermon, but only to initiate the exploration of the Scripture.

His exegetical opening then leads to the group's discussion of the meaning of this passage for today. What questions does it raise? What problems does it present? What aspects of it need to be clarified before contemporary lay people can find it helpful? The group shares with the minister in defining a preaching theme based on the passage. Members suggest situations in their current life to which it might apply, issues on which it throws light, and experiences that might have illustrative value in relation to it.

Against the background of this discussion the minister then continues his preparation. As is understood by all, the sermon that emerges is the minister's responsibility, and he is not obligated to echo the opinions of members of the group. Yet in his development of the sermon he has the advantage of insights into the mind of the group and into its needs, which otherwise he might have missed. Consequently, the sermon that emerges has more opportunity to make contact with people where they are. Also, the group process may serve to clarify the minister's thinking and give reality to the priesthood of believers within the parish. And the members of the group who have participated in the preparation hear the sermon with a depth of attention scarcely possible for the uninvolved.

In larger churches where the sermon seminar is used, the basic method is the same. The chief difference lies in the possibility that a larger group of participants may need to be divided into small working groups. The session begins in the same way: the member of the ministerial staff who is to preach the sermon under consideration makes the opening exegetical statement. Necessary clarifying questions are then dealt with. After that the group divides into clusters of six or eight persons each to continue the discussion. The preaching minister visits about among the groups to get the trend of their discussion, and in the closing minutes of the hour there are reports from the groups, listing questions, issues, and illuminating experiences. In use in various places over a period of more than two decades, this method has served to fit preparation helpfully into the opinion-change network.[11]

The Talkback Session

Other models continue the two-way exchange between minister and congregation after the sermon has been delivered. In some parishes a *talkback session,* or forum discussion, occurs every Sunday; in others, once a month or on some similar periodical basis. Some churches incorporate the "talkback" into the service of worship; others close the service and move to a social hall for the informal discussion. Cards are sometimes placed in the pews for the convenience of listeners in articulating their understanding of the sermon. Such a card may be as simple as a blank page in the bulletin, headed with an invitation to use this space for notes on the sermon. Or it may provide spaces in which to write the sermon's text, its main idea, and the supporting ideas that stood out. A helpful card form, devised by Henry B. Adams,[12] is shown in Figure 8.

Such cards and note-taking serve a dual purpose. They help the listener to take a more active role in the two-way communication, making at least these overt responses as the sermon unfolds. And they lend assistance to memory, both in the talkback session and in later recall of whatever may have been helpful in the message. For congregations whose talkback sessions occur less frequently—once a month, for instance—the cards serve to bring back into focus matters of interest in sermons from past Sundays.

The talkback session, or forum discussion of the sermon, has a multiple usefulness. (*a*) It helps to verify impressions; participants state what they understood the sermon to be saying. Others can then respond with their understandings. Out of the exchange comes mutual clarification and the deepening of im-

Figure 8. Listener's Card

WHAT THIS SERMON MEANS TO ME

A sermon is a mutual experience we all share, something that happens among us. Your understanding of the sermon will not be exactly like anyone else's, but it is an important part of the total meanings that make up the message today.

Try to digest the sermon into three sentences below. Put down what you can, no matter how incomplete. Try to word the ideas as you understand them in terms of your own life.

1. The problem or need with which the sermon was concerned. *Word it as a question.*

2. The truth developed in the sermon in answer to the question. *Word it as an assertion.*

3. The response to the above truth which the sermon urged. *Word it as an invitation.*

pressions. (*b*) Discussion supplements the sermon; listeners can raise questions about points they did not fully understand. Other listeners as well as the preacher can then contribute to the further explanation. In the process, the sermon grows more enlightening and convincing. (*c*) Objections can be voiced; where they are based on misunderstanding, points can be cleared. Both the preacher and other members of the group can throw further light on the matter at issue. Even where the objector remains unconvinced, his disagreement becomes less troublesome because it has been heard and he has personally been received with grace and acceptance. (*d*) The selective aspect of perception and memory noted earlier in this chapter can be at least partially overcome. What has been tuned out or misunderstood because of preconceptions may very possibly come to attention again in the discussion. There is thus a second opportunity for it to make its rightful impression.

The Feedback Team

What has been called the *feedback team* provides another form of response to the sermon, designed to serve a somewhat different end but partaking of many of the values of the talkback session. The team is a small group, numbering from six to nine persons and generally changing periodically. It meets for from forty minutes to an hour after the service. For the limited number of participants, many of the clarifying functions of the forum just discussed can accrue. The purpose, however, is to help the minister to become a better communicator by responding to feedback.

Experience indicates that such groups express themselves more freely when the minister is not present. Their discussion is recorded on tape, and it is understood that the minister will listen carefully to what is said. There is more revealing discussion, however, when he is not visibly seated in the circle.

The group generally meets without a designated leader. Members of the group have been carefully briefed on the purpose for which they are gathered, and they have before them a set of suggestive questions to key their discussion. One of their number has been designated as convener, to call the group to order and start the tape recorder. Beyond that, such leadership as may be needed emerges from the group as it proceeds. Questions that elicit the feedback are generally variants of those which grew out of Reuel Howe's experience with the method at the Institute for Advanced Pastoral Studies.[13] As adapted in one parish, they read: What did the preacher say to you? (Not, What did he say? but, What did you hear?) What difference, if any, do you think the sermon will make in your life (or was it of passing, theoretical interest only)? In what ways did the

preacher's method, language, illustrations, and delivery help or
hinder your hearing of the message? What relation, if any, did
you see between the sermon and the worship service? Is there
anything else you want to say to the preacher (including things
you have always wanted to say to preachers but never had the
occasion)?

Among those who have worked with feedback teams there
is general consensus regarding their value. Lay participants say
that (*a*) the feedback team has given them a sense of active
participation in the preaching encounter, which has transformed
all subsequent hearing of sermons; and (*b*) in the group discussion they found a sense of the saving reality of the Word
never experienced in their less involved individual listening.
Ministers report that (*a*) they have learned much about themselves as communicators and about the things that do and do
not communicate successfully; that (*b*) study of the feedback
tapes has helped them to know their people and their needs in
ways available through no other channel; and (*c*) in instances
when the feedback has been used for the expression of hostility
toward the preacher and his message, this venting of resentment
helped to make it less harmful and rendered the parishioner
more open to *hear* what the preacher was saying on subsequent
occasions.

An Integrated Network

In orienting preaching to its distinctive role in a multichannel
milieu we have seen it as occupying a place of special importance among the many ministries of communication, exerting
a decisive effect on all other functions through which the minister seeks to serve. Preaching most effectively overcomes the
handicaps that haunt the spoken word (*a*) when it takes its
place in an integrated network of communicative relationships,
some of which we have surveyed in this chapter; (*b*) when it
emphasizes good news, placing exhortations to change in the
context of a gospel emphasis; and (*c*) when it serves a teaching

function that makes ample provision for two-way communication through such methods as the sermon seminar, the talkback forum, and the feedback team.

PROBES

1. Amplified treatment of methods of opening channels for two-way communication with the sermon may be found in several sources. Browne Barr, *Parish Back Talk* (Abingdon Press, 1964), deals with the sermon seminar. Reuel L. Howe, *Partners in Preaching* (The Seabury Press, 1967), Ch. 10, puts the feedback team in context in Howe's version of dialogical preaching. Wallace E. Fisher, *Preaching and Parish Renewal* (Abingdon Press, 1966), pp. 203–206, describes a monthly form of talkback forum and suggests a useful type of card for the listener's note-taking. Dow Kirkpatrick, *Six Days—and Sunday: A Pew-Pulpit Dialogue* (Abingdon Press, 1968), pp. 5–9, applies two-way communication to a special series of topical sermons. William D. Thompson, *A Listener's Guide to Preaching* (Abingdon Press, 1966), provides a practical pocket paperback manual for ministers and lay people seeking ways to advance the pulpit ministry as a genuine communicative exchange.

2. The concept of "opinion leaders" bears a close relation to the previously noted influence of primary groups. This makes doubly startling the sociological data on many congregations, placing them in the category of " 'religious audiences' rather than primary groups." Surveys indicate that although 29 percent of all Protestants said that "three to five" of their closest friends were members of their congregation, 36 percent responded "none" to the same question.[14] This is a point where pastoral leadership and preaching effectiveness are interdependent: welding persons into a primary group is a pastoral task; it is also a preaching necessity if the pulpit is to have lasting influence. Consider and discuss practical ways in which the congregation you know best may be made more fully a matrix of primary group life.

CHAPTER 7

Interpreting the
Biblical Message

Productive preaching gives a central place to Biblical interpretation. Christian faith rests on the Bible as its normative guide. A preacher proclaiming Jesus Christ as Savior and Lord is driven to the Bible as the one source of all that we know of his life, ministry, and message. Preaching in the name of God as known through his mighty acts, one turns to the Bible for understanding of his dealings with Israel, and from these one learns how to look for God's presence in history and contemporary life. In the Old Testament the preacher finds the background, and in the New Testament the fullest expression, of the radically new faith and life that Jesus brought to the world. To give thrust to a message that is distinctively Christian, the preacher inevitably takes his stance as a Biblical interpreter.

Not only historical and theological imperatives make this essential; it is a foundational communicative necessity as well. No matter how urgent the minister's convictions concerning the contemporary scene, no matter how eager he may be to get on with present tasks in the world around him, he will be hindered by heightened barriers of role-image conflict unless he is perceived as a careful and credible interpreter of the Bible. He is cast in the interpreter's role by listener expectations. This is how the church understands his professional specialty. When he was ordained, a Bible was placed in his hands as he received the solemn commission: "Take thou authority . . . to preach the Word of God, and to administer the holy Sacraments in the congregation." [1] In such a setting, any contemporary message to which a preacher wishes to give persuasive thrust will be heard with difficulty, if at all, unless the assembled faithful can clearly perceive the message as an outgrowth of valid interpretation of Biblical insights.

Acceptance of this role is no handicap to the lively timeliness of the skilled and imaginative interpreter. The Biblical documents, timelessly colorful and dramatic, can supply the preached word with that piquant interest which they have provided for novelists and playwrights across the years. No preacher who must regularly speak to the same congregation week by week can spin out of his own intellect materials to give truth, significance, and force to such a ministry; but the preacher who regularly draws on the resources of the Bible, in living contact with contemporary life, will not lack materials for a message. To neglect this wealth is to court bankruptcy. To draw on it is to work from "an amazing compendium of every kind of situation in human experience with the garnered wisdom of the ages to help in meeting them." [2]

Danger of lost contact with this renewing stream perennially threatens the church. At the end of a five-year period that had seen Bible distribution in the United States increase by 140 percent, to nearly ten million copies a year, a survey showed little popular acquaintance with the content of the book. Although more than 80 percent of the people, asked whether the Bible is "a great piece of literature" or "the revealed word of God," declared for the latter, 50 percent could not name even one of the first four books of the New Testament.[3] In the face of such a gap between the espoused norm of our faith and popular information about it, the preaching office is confronted by both mandate and opportunity to supply interpretation that will help to renew the church's knowledge.

Building Hermeneutic Bridges

For many a modern, the Bible is a closed book, chiefly for want of such interpretation. "What do these ancients have to say to me?" a late-twentieth-century businessman asks. "They rode camels; I travel by jet. They fought with swords and spears; I have to cope with multiple-warhead nuclear missiles. They lived in a familiar world, unchanging from father to son to grandson; I'm hurtled through a world that has changed more in my lifetime than it did from Caesar's day to the year of my birth. What could *they* know about my world? What can they say to *me?*"

To such inquiry it must be answered that, read superficially, the Biblical documents can achieve only limited communication across such a gap. If these writers issued only laws and propositions keyed to their culture and world view, they speak now with restricted relevance. Yet, amid all changes, some basic realities remain stable. Universal human experiences tie all generations together: birth and growth, with its struggles; joy and pain; success and frustration; temptation and victory or the pangs of guilt; forgiveness and its liberating power; the necessity to establish and maintain some kind of orderly governance in society; the agonies of conquest and the ecstasy of liberation; and those dread ultimates—death, bereavement, and shattering grief. For these universals the Biblical documents have a vast storehouse of experience and guiding insight, although the modern reader must bridge bewildering differences in the cultural forms in which they are clothed. Building the bridges is the hermeneutic task of the preacher.

Light falls on this undertaking from its analogy with legal hermeneutic. For hermeneutic—interpretation—is the purpose of the judicial system. The courts exist, we commonly say, to interpret the law. Lawyers, judges, juries, and all the erudite structure of the legal system, culminating in the Supreme Court, are focused on the function of interpreting the law and applying it to the specifics of individual cases. However, to say this is to miss the essentially human dimension of the matter; for the real objective is to work out the intricacies of tangled human situations. When a problem becomes too complicated for litigants to solve—a disputed boundary, a defaulted contract, a contested inheritance, an alleged crime—the legal system is brought to bear upon the solution. A sore and troubled aspect of human relations needs interpretation that will allow life to go on, and the court is the interpreter. Interpretation of *law* is secondary and instrumental; interpretation of *life* is the primary need. Yet unless the law is interpreted faithfully, its interpretation of life goes astray.

Biblical hermeneutic is similarly related to life's ultimate issues. In order to interpret the Bible we learn languages, develop skill in critical methodology, buttress understanding with historical research and archaeological data, develop departments of Biblical interpretation in our seminaries, and amass libraries of commentary and other hermeneutic resources. Yet to put it thus is to miss the life-dimension. "I came that they may have life," said Jesus, "and have it abundantly" (John 10:10). The goal of those who interpret him must not stray from his own. Our tangled life needs interpretation in order to have its embittered relationships set right, injustices rectified, guilts forgiven, differences reconciled, meaninglessness lighted up with purpose, shackles of enslavement broken, pain conquered, grief healed, death met with victory. The whole system of Biblical interpretation is brought to bear upon the task of interpreting our life. Interpreting the text is not the real goal, but a means of drawing on matchless resources of illumination for shadowed places in human affairs. As courts interpret life truly only when they are painstakingly faithful in interpreting the law, Christian preaching and teaching interpret life with healing wholeness only when they faithfully interpret the Biblical message.

Preaching encodes its message truly only after it has carefully decoded what has come to us through the Biblical documents. Here lies the problem of the modern hearer. For the

Biblical message was not only encoded in ancient languages that must be translated; its encoding occurred in a culture so unlike ours that, even when its words are accurately translated into the modern vernacular, its customs, world view, and axiomatic assumptions are often all but impenetrable for modern men. To decode the message so that across this cultural chasm we comprehend what the ancient writers were saying, and then to encode *that intended meaning* in imagery that can accurately convey it to men immersed in contemporary culture, is the formidable assignment of the preacher.

We deal seriously with the printed text, but our real concern is with events. Something significant happened, which gave birth to the text. Something of like significance needs to happen again. As Gerhard Ebeling memorably put it, "The word that once happened and in happening became the text must again become word with the help of the text and thus happen as interpreting word." [4] The interpreter is commissioned to penetrate the text in search of its own intention. He is not a reporter of history, repeating what the text said; he is a contemporary messenger, proclaiming in the symbols of his time what the text proclaimed in the images of another day. "Its aim," said Ebeling, "is that there should be further proclamation. . . . Proclamation that has taken place is to become proclamation that takes place." [5] Tangled and imprisoned life is to be illuminated and set free. "The text by means of the sermon becomes a hermeneutic aid in the understanding of present experience." [6]

Making Accurate Exegesis

Because the preacher's goal is communication—making effective contact with another's meanings—his sermon need not show all his workshop steps in decoding the Biblical truth. He must deal with his listeners where he finds them. Only such parts of his ferreting out of the meaning and intentionality of the text as will contribute to contact with the hearer's meanings should be incorporated into the finished message. Yet, before the message can be constructed, a diligent search must guide the preacher to what the text is saying. As the hermeneutic task interprets across the culture gap what the text *means*, the exegetical endeavor uncovers, as accurately as possible, what the text really *says*.

Here the preacher shares the responsibility that falls on all translators. Walter Kaufmann, who produced the rich 1970 translation of Martin Buber's *I and Thou*, wrote in the prologue: "As a translator I have no right to use the text confronting me as an object with which I may take liberties. It is not there for me to play with or manipulate. I am not to use it as a point of departure, or as anything else. It is the voice of a person that needs me. I am there to help him speak." [7] What human honesty demands of the translator of the work of a modern author, honesty and his sense of a divine call must require of one who speaks for God: "I am to help him speak."

The exegete's search for the plain truth of what a text says cannot be reproduced in detail in such a book as this; yet we need to review in brief summary some of the essential steps without which a preacher cannot deal with his Scriptural sources.

1. He must begin by hearing the text in its own *Biblical setting*. Quoting another out of context—a trick of unscrupulous demagogues—gains nothing in honesty or truth when applied to the Bible. The preacher must relate the text to the Biblical book or document of which it is a part, seeking to determine how it contributed to the message and intent of that book. He must inquire into its historical setting, to whom it was addressed, by whom, and under what conditions. He will ask: What were the issues at stake? How did the people of its own time understand it?

2. Having oriented the text to its setting, he will seek the most accurate *understanding of its language* available to him. If he has skill in the ancient languages, he will go back of all translations to confront it in its original tongue. At the very least, he will read it comparatively in several different modern translations. Sermons based on the English phraseology of one

translation sometimes have novelty and charm; they are not likely to be notably true. The unsupported phrasing of a single translation is very probably an eccentricity produced by the accident of an English sentence. One translation may render the original more incisively or colorfully than do others, but if it gives a meaning which only its form of words conveys, it is suspect. The preacher not skilled in Hebrew and Greek will do well to base no sermon on an understanding of the Biblical text that departs from a clear consensus among able translators.

3. He will pursue his search for linguistic accuracy a step further, seeking such light on the meaning of the text as he can gain from a *study of its syntax*. In the process he will examine the backgrounds of key words in the text. How are these same words used elsewhere in the Bible? What light do these other uses throw upon the meaning here? Do these key words have connotations in the ancient Near Eastern cultures that are different from our connotations? For this step in his work he will be wise to consult the best Bible dictionaries available to him and to use such tools as handbooks of word studies or such lexicons of the original languages as his linguistic skills make available to him.

4. His understanding of the text needs illumination by discerning its *literary type*. If it is poetry, it will be more accurately understood by allowance for the figurative language common to poets of all ages, and by seeking the light thrown on the meaning by such peculiar devices of Hebrew poetry as its constant use of parallelism. If it is parable, he will guard against the tendency of modern readers to allegorize, and will focus rather on the one key idea that the whole parable was designed to articulate. If it is narrative, he will search for its main thread of meaning, and he will ask: How did this fit the overall intent of the ancient narrator? What can I properly suppose he was attempting to accomplish by the telling of this story? If it is apocalyptic, he will bear in mind such peculiarities of this type of writing as its strong dualism, its emphasis on a dramatic end of the world, its common use of the name of some honored

figure as a pseudonym for its author, and its building of content out of symbolic visions, predicted woes, the manipulation of symbolic numbers, and a stress on angels, demons, and other figurative devices. Only as he decodes such literary conventions can he arrive at the meaning of his text.

5. From historical, linguistic, and literary study, the preacher will move on to a more *personal confrontation.* How does God seek for men through this passage? he will ask. How does he search *me?* Being who I am, where I am, with my limitations and talents, my problems and victories, my sins and my sharing in God's grace, how does this text speak to me? Am I letting it find me *now?* In such introspection he will seek to understand the text in its important dimension as a part of God's ongoing dialogue with men.

6. Against all this background, he will attempt to *assess the dynamics* of the text. What are the forces at work within it? What movement runs through it? Is an issue joined? If so, what is its resolution? Are opposing forces at work? If so, what tensions develop and what is the outcome? A static view of a text is as inadequate as a single frame from a motion picture. We need to know the direction and quality of the movement; and a sharp statement of the forces, tensions, and outcome is an effective way to discover this essential dynamic.

7. When the preacher has done his own hard work with the text, he needs to correct and amplify his findings by *reading the best commentaries* at his command. To begin with the commentaries will not serve this purpose. What he finds by his own search is vivid and alive for him; what he reads in commentaries before he has exhausted his personal resources is secondhand. If he begins with such reading, he is not likely to advance beyond it. If he neglects such reading, he may fall into needless inaccuracies or deprive himself of wealth he could have shared. If he does such reading at the end of his own exegetical struggle, it will correct him where he went astray, fill in much that he missed, balance what he saw with bias—and do all this without stifling his own imagination, creativity, and sense of reality.

The exegetical question (What does the text really *say?*) and the hermeneutic question (What does the text *mean* when lifted out of its culture into ours?) comprise the exciting first steps toward the making of a worthy sermon.

The Bible Book Course

Biblical interpretation needs planned continuity. Understanding of the Christian faith has suffered from the fragmentation born of long habituation to a relatively planless spontaneity in the choice of texts. The preacher who will work from a careful plan, which puts him under the necessities of a systematic progression through Biblical materials, can go far toward building a sense of wholeness in the mind of his congregation and advancing his own knowledge of the Scriptures and the message that runs through them.

One approach to such continuity is the presentation, during one or two periods each year, of a course of sermons on a selected book of the Bible. A period of about three months is best adapted to such course continuity. During these twelve or thirteen weeks, the preacher can make his way through one of the Gospels, an epistle, or one of the prophetic books, developing its main themes, dealing with problems in our life that parallel those with which it was chiefly concerned, exploring its principal literary modes, getting to know some of its memorable characters. In three months he cannot treat everything in any major book, but its main thrust can reach him and his people with new persuasive power.

If it is done hand to mouth, such a course will be thin. For at least the three months that precede the period of the course, the preacher needs to study the book from which he intends to preach. He will read and reread it, outline it, and read one or two of the best books he can find about it. Thus he will come to it with some sense of its historical provenance, its critical problems, and its theological impact. It would be even better to give the book a major place in his study a year in advance.

One useful way for the preacher to conduct such study is to focus on the chosen book for his devotional reading during a major part of the year. Day by day he can read consecutively in the book, each day a passage that sets forth the next complete incident or idea. By such measurement, the units will vary in length from a sentence or two to several paragraphs, and they will have cumulative meaning. Of each passage, the minister will ask two questions. First, there is the exegetical inquiry: What does this passage *say?* Second, there is the hermeneutic and existential quest: What does the passage mean to *me?* He will write his findings daily in his notebook in diary fashion. In the process, his knowledge of the book will grow, and God will guide his personal growth. As the time to prepare the intended course of sermons approaches, the minister will review his notebook. He will find that much of the material is of passing interest, having already served its purpose in the preliminary study. Here and there he will find a page that glows with possibilities. Collecting a dozen or thirteen of these, he will restudy them, formulate from them sermon themes, arrange them in an order that will best fit the calendar, and proceed to the weekly development of the sermons.

The values of such continuity are many. (*a*) It gives cumulative impact to the pulpit message, each sermon buttressed by the others in the course. (*b*) It confirms the preacher in systematic disciplines of Bible study that enrich his mind and enhance his growing effectiveness over the years. (*c*) It encourages systematic Bible-reading among members of the congregation. Announcing the sermons for the given period, the minister can invite his people to make the chosen book a part of their own reading during that time. A considerable number will respond; and the reading, illumined by the sermons, will be a rewarding experience. (*d*) It can build a Biblical point of view in a congregation, as at least one or two such courses each year take the members through a growing area of Biblical literature, to which they are exposed with some measure of wholeness. (*e*) Along the way, the alert preacher will deal with many contemporary issues, not as subjects of his arbitrary choice but as raised by the book itself; and this fact will place controversial issues in a new and natural context, which makes listeners more ready to hear what the preacher needs to say.

Continuity via the Lectionary

An alternative approach to Biblical continuity can be made through sustained use of a good lectionary as the basis for the choice of texts. In some denominations this practice is the expected procedure. Where it is not, a sadly abridged Bible becomes the actual working tool of the pulpit. A survey of a devotional book[8] produced without a lectionary provides an instance. Intended for use by ministers and other church leaders, it was compiled by asking theologians, teachers, and others who could command the respect of such an audience each to supply the daily devotional fare for a week. Each used his own themes and chose his own Scriptures. With 365 days to be covered, 201 of the Bible readings involved repetition of only 66 favored passages, which were repeated from two to seven times each. Such is the imbalance that almost inevitably occurs, even among sophisticated interpreters, unless some device is employed to increase the range.

A good lectionary is such a device. In systematic and scholarly fashion, it leads a congregation through greater areas of Scriptural concern than most ministers would discover alone. The lectionaries of the major denominations are designed to engage the worshiper, in the course of a year, with materials from every book of the Bible. Thus personal biases can be overcome and some balanced Biblical diet provided.

Within this assured wholeness the preacher is left with great areas of freedom. He chooses his text from Old Testament lesson, Epistle, or Gospel. If he develops a sentence text, he has a wide choice within these three passages; or he may work from a whole pericope; or the appointed passage may lead to treatment of a larger section of the book from which it is selected; or a character central to one of the passages may be studied biographically, with a focus in the incident or issue treated in the text. Thus the lectionary invites the preacher's creative imagination to devise a variety of approaches to a wide assortment of materials, providing means of constantly sustained interest.

The unity and progression of the preaching program that can result is integrated by the drama of the Christian year, to which every good lectionary is keyed. Each liturgical season has its own theological center of concern, and the Scriptures within the season are those which the church's cumulative experience has found most appropriate to this message. In this dynamic progression, all the major emphases of the gospel receive Biblical statement in the round of the seasons.

As in the case of the Bible book course of sermons, preaching from the lectionary comes to its best only through planning. The preacher studies ahead in the seasons before him. For each season he visualizes some theme or series of themes to be developed. For one period of weeks he may follow the Old Testament lessons, for another the Epistles, for a third the Gospels. Thus within the total continuity of the lectionary year, special series may emerge. Finding his way deeply into these Scriptures by a method similar to that used in his study of the book chosen for a three-month course, he finds their wealth and shares it with his people.

The Preacher as a Biblical Teacher

The Biblical rootlessness of churchmen who hold orthodox views *about* the Bible but have little knowledge *of* it can be reversed by a pulpit that gives itself to careful, systematic Biblical interpretation. In such a ministry the preacher can be guided to a message possessing authenticity and depth scarcely obtainable in any other way. Such preaching gains credibility by fulfilling the role and image expectations inherent in the church's understanding of the ministerial office. At the same time it can draw on sources of dramatic interest and power to which the world's creative literature perennially returns. While it is accomplishing the important educational task of leading a congregation to more sustained and informed reading of the Bible, such preaching can place contemporary life in a large and truth-sustaining perspective, meeting controversial issues as a matter of course, since they are raised by the materials studied.

The minister who achieves all this will need to be not only a careful student of the Bible but a teacher as well. Chapter 8 will deal with ways in which a teaching pulpit can strengthen the church's witness.

PROBES

1. Excellent guidance in practical methodology for informed and varied Biblical preaching is provided by Dwight E. Stevenson, *In the Biblical Preacher's Workshop* (Abingdon Press, 1967). Gerhard Ebeling's helpful theological grounding of the hermeneutic enterprise is detailed in his *Word and Faith* (tr. by James W. Leitch; Fortress Press, 1963). See also *The New Hermeneutic,* ed. by James M. Robinson and John B. Cobb, Jr. (Harper & Row, Publishers, Inc., 1964). Merrill R. Abbey, *The Word Interprets Us* (Abingdon Press, 1967), is a handbook of hermeneutic as applied to preaching. For a commentary on one major lectionary, designed to suggest preaching approaches to its readings for the year, see Merrill R. Abbey, *The Shape of the Gospel: Interpreting the Bible Through the Christian Year* (Abingdon Press, 1970).

2. You might begin to build a preaching continuity on the basis of the lectionary of your own denomination. Study the lessons appointed for a liturgical season some weeks or months in the future, and select a sequence of readings—Old Testament lessons, Epistles, or Gospels. Use your daily Bible study hours over a period of time to explore these passages exegetically and to let them search you devotionally and existentially, recording

your reflections in a notebook. When you have worked your way through the passages in this fashion, go back over your notebook, formulating preaching themes for the approaching liturgical season. Continue to accumulate your reflections in your growing notebook, and out of this firsthand treasury of material preach the series for the season.

3. As an alternative, or for use at a later time, make a similar study of a Bible book, formulate themes from it, and prepare a course of sermons for a period of approximately three months. The Gospel According to Mark—because of its basic material, its brevity, and its vividness—would lend itself to a first venture in such continuity.

CHAPTER 8

Teaching a Witnessing Church

That the Christian message is communicated to the world through the witnessing action of the church does not detract from the vitality of the spoken message. Articulate leaders still count heavily, but in today's mass society it is groups gathered around firmly held convictions that make the moving difference. To be heard, a leader must consolidate the witness of his own group. In the critical closing decades of the twentieth century, Christian influence depends upon preaching that instructs the church's witness.

In business, industry, and the professions, in the polling booth, amid changing mores, lay people make the crucial decisions. In their thought and action, will the Christian faith find voice? J. W. Stevenson reflects on a decision at the village hall in a small Scottish parish. "The minister of the parish was not there. . . . But the Church was there. Every one of them was a member of the Church; some of them were elders of the Church. But there was no voice of the Church there, with this decision on them and the voice of the Deceiver there, urging them, 'Would it work, would it work, would it benefit them, would it serve their interests?' . . . It was some of those men who needed to be the voice of the Church, putting what seemed workable in its proper place with what was commanded. Some of them should have been prepared, in the only way Christian

men can be prepared." [1] Their preparation required able theological teaching, and this could have been their minister's vital
civic contribution—but it needed to be done long before the
crisis arose.

The minister need not withdraw from the scene of action. As
a citizen, he shares the rights and responsibilities of other
citizens. His distinctive role, however, and his most powerful
strategy, will be found in his work as a teacher. If lay men and
women are to be "the voice of the church, putting what seems
workable in its proper place with what is commanded," they
need careful guidance in the structure and meaning of Christian
teachings as these relate to workaday affairs. By training and
commission, the minister is cast in the teacher's role. Preaching
affords him a matchless opportunity. Promoters of other ideolo-
gies must fight for a hearing; the minister, week by week, is
given his. Richard Baxter's seventeenth-century demand is still
timely: "If you would not teach men, what do you do in the
pulpit?" [2]

This chapter centers attention upon practical aspects of
preaching as it teaches a witnessing church.

The Theological Dimension of Preaching

In his parish, the minister is a theologian-in-residence, whose
distinctive function it is to help men understand the content
of their faith and its points of intersection with their everyday
affairs. There is force in Reuel Howe's reply to ministers who
"complain that they do not have a speciality, and are the only
generalists left in a specialist society." They have created that
plight, he contends, by trying to do many things better done
by lay people: to be "counselors, therapists, group specialists,
community organizers, administrators, demonstrators." He
points to people in business and the professions who are ready
to carry the action programs. They are asking for help "with
the religious and theological meanings of their lives." "This,"

he adds, "is the clergyman's specialty and must be increasingly so, as we move into the future." [3]

By way of illustration, Howe reports the change in an industrial enterprise when its head came to see the practical thrust of Christian teachings he had espoused without full understanding. The executive had raised the question how his faith could affect his business, and Howe replied by inquiring what doctrine of man guided his business operations. In the lively exploration of doctrine that ensued, the man moved, little by little, to a less autocratic administration, which allowed employees more freedom for personal initiative, responsibility, and growth. Not all of the work of bringing about such change can be done in the pulpit, but preaching *can* raise issues and offer basic instruction on which other teaching devices and pastoral care can follow through.

Moral values have no lasting foundations in moralism. In all that matters decisively, men act out their response, not to what they are told they *ought* to do, but to what they believe to be "most important and most real." [4] Pronouncements about personal or social ethics often fall on deaf ears because those to whom they are addressed have not been helped to see them as inevitable outgrowths of their faith's deepest truth concerning the basic nature of the world and of our common life. A significant modern British preacher was wont to assert that "doctrines must be preached practically and duties doctrinally." [5]

Only such preaching makes a difference, because only it is true to its gospel. At its deepest, the Christian message is neither an imperative, "we ought," nor a conditional subjunctive, e.g., "If only we would do thus and so, we could attain this desired reward." The gospel is a strong indicative: "This is how life is; this is what God has done; this is what you were made to be." Idealism is not only impotent, it is unbiblical. The Scriptures do not hold up shining ideals by which men ought to live; they report events and declare realities. Even the Ten Commandments root in the reiteration of the reality of God's mighty acts and abiding grace: "I am the LORD your God, who brought you out of the land of Egypt, out of the house of bondage" (Ex. 20:2). All the ensuing imperatives of the Decalogue stem from this indicative. It is precisely because our time needs a rebirth of ethical insight as applied to personal and social relations that we need a rediscovery of the teaching pulpit that powers imperatives with the gospel's strong indicatives.

Whether the preacher starts with a doctrine or a contemporary issue, the two must meet. Ecology, for example, is the business of the pulpit, not for the reasons of generalized humanism that make it a popular concern, but because it is the critical point of junction of our life with great doctrines: the earth as God's creation, which he loves, and the care of the earth as man's stewardship under God. Likewise, the maladjustments of personality or human relations are the business of the pulpit, not because the pulpit is a forum for psychological teaching but because such maladjustments are symptoms of the human predicament; because we are enmeshed in sin as separation from God, ourselves, and our fellow men; and because there is healing. There is healing in forgiveness and all that Christian faith has understood as "justification," and in that growth into maturity in Christ which the great word "sanctification" implies. The pulpit has a distinctive teaching task that gives men's dealings with emergent issues an indispensable depth and power not available elsewhere.

Avoiding the "I Told Them" Fallacy

Fulfillment of this function requires that the preacher be not only an informed theologian but an able teacher as well. Teaching is more than the statement of doctrines. The "I told them" fallacy[6] will quickly ensnare the preacher who expects to "give" his people the truth on any doctrine or issue. The frustrated young man who despairs of the possibility of a useful parish ministry protests against the willful social blindness of the church. "Preaching is a hopeless undertaking," he declares. "My people persist in the old mind-set, though I've told them the Christian position in a whole series of sermons."

The "I told them" fallacy roots in the assumption that meanings inhere in messages and, in the last analysis, in words. It does not take seriously the way in which words change meanings, from time to time, place to place, person to person. James Joyce pictures the absolutizing of words, in the musings of the young Stephen Dedalus. "When anyone prayed to God and said Dieu," Stephen reflected, "then God knew at once that it was a French person that was praying. But though there were different names for God in all the different languages in the world and God understood what all the people who prayed said in their different languages still God remained always the same God and God's real name was God." [7]

Meanings cannot be locked into words with such finality. Dictionaries are properly understood not as regulative, but as historical and reportorial. They document how words have been used and are being used. They deal mainly with what we might call "public" meanings. For each of us, words have our own "private" meanings as well. In more formal terminology, we speak of *denotative* and *connotative* meanings or, with S. I. Hayakawa, *extensional* and *intensional* meanings. *Denotative* and *extensional* are the terms we use to indicate the "pointing" quality of a word. With these we designate the object, concept, quality or action; *connotative* and *intensional,* on the other hand, are the terms we use to designate the personal associations that have gathered around a word.

Since preaching and other instances of ministerial communication are often highly personal expressions of one's convictions, addressed to others in matters personally important to them, these personalized, connotative or intensional definitions of words carry a heavy cargo of meaning that can advance or handicap useful communication. Sensitivity to these meanings, for oneself and others, becomes crucial.

When we neglect this fluctuating quality of words we are easy victims of the " 'I told them' fallacy," supposing that mean-

ings go automatically with messages and that those who have
heard the message must thereby have received the meaning.

Meanings Are in Persons

Meanings are functions of persons, not properties of messages.
They may be evoked by messages, yet they have their only real
existence in persons, not in the messages themselves. The message, "God loves you with a freely given love; he does not ask
you to earn the right to be loved, nor does he withdraw his
love when you fail him," seems clear enough. But a man who,
deserted by his parents in his childhood, had fallen victim to
repeated rejections by persons from whom he expected acceptance, until he isolated himself and anticipated exclusion as a
kind of self-fulfilling prophecy, could not hear the words with
their expected clarity. Meanings that had accumulated in his
mind and emotions so blocked and colored the meaning intended
by the words in their usual Christian connotation that reaching
him with the message became a matter of long and difficult
pastoral dealing with him as a person.

We do not hear a message simply with our ears or our cognitive powers. We hear it with our perception of its full context,
with our previous understandings, with our attitudes, our estimate of its relation to our place in our primary groups, and a
host of other factors deeply embedded in our personal being.
No communicator can transmit *meanings;* he can only transmit
messages designed to evoke desired and intended meanings.

Yet meanings can be learned. If it is true that meanings
already present act as filters, which block or distort meanings
intended by a message, it is also true that messages can have
some part in helping us to change old meanings and learn new
ones. In such learning, a new connection is made between present experience and meanings already held, until the old meanings are seen in a new light. The man who could not *hear* the
meaning of the love of God may need a long-tested experience
of being loved with faithfulness and acceptance. In addition he

may need help in reliving past traumatic experiences until he can accept them in a new light. In the process, the new meaning may lay hold upon aspects of the old, inhibiting meanings and transform them.

"Meanings," says Berlo, "are our interpretations, the receiver-and-source behaviors that we perform internally." [8] Thus meanings are processes taking place in persons. They attach themselves to personal experiences and can change with changing experience. We cannot "give" others the truth; we can only help them learn. Their active involvement is imperative. The truth we would explore with them must *meet their meanings*.

Pulpit Power in Learning Principles

Such methods as the sermon seminar, talkback session, and feedback team, which we have already explored (Chapter 6), are designed to facilitate this meeting of meanings. We need also to guide our preaching by what has been learned in other disciplines about factors that strengthen learning.

1. *Learning is strengthened when an experience is repeated frequently in a way rewarding to the learner.* In experimental psychology this refers to repetition of the same stimulus with rewarded response. In preaching it gives rise to repeated statement and restatement of a central idea around which cumulative associations gather, with a rewarding growth of insight. Harry Emerson Fosdick is one of many who have derived great power as teaching preachers from apt use of this device.

In his sermon "The Means Determine the End," Fosdick stated the main idea forcefully in the first paragraph. Citing the common futility of resolutions that set out blithely for high goals, he added, "Our wills cannot deal directly with ends, only with means, so that, making idealistic decisions about ends and letting the means take care of themselves, we wake up to discover that the means have determined the ends." [9]

As the sermon unfolded, he kept this idea steadily in evidence. At the end of the second paragraph he said of the failure of ideals publicly espoused, "The means used are not pertinent to the ends sought, and the means determine the ends." A page later he underscored that: "We never can get peace by unpeaceful methods, or democracy by undemocratic methods, or liberty by illiberal methods. Always, the means we use must partake of the quality of the goal we seek." Turning to more intimate needs, he declared: "We cannot get lovely homes by unlovely means or faithful homes by unfaithful methods. In a family the means we use must partake of the quality of the goals we seek." Two paragraphs later he added, "But in the church, too, the means determine the ends, and we should not let the foolishness of preaching blind us to the truth of this similitude in the spiritual realm." Six times in the remaining portion of the sermon, the basic theme statement is repeated, yet frequency of repetition does not become monotony, for it is *rewarded* frequency. Not only is there charm in the style within which the repetition is set; there is a continuous gathering of insights around the theme, as one sees one area of his experience after another illuminated.

2. *Isolation of the desired relationship of stimulus and response strengthens the learning process.* If distracting stimuli to which the learner attends can be reduced or eliminated, the probability of achieving the desired end is increased. The preacher has opportunity to apply this principle at least within the structured limits of a worship service. Outside distractions are shut out by the setting. Yet in many a service the worshiper comes to the sermon already jaded by the number of miscellaneous announcements, exhortations to assorted good causes, and other distractions that have demanded attention. Often, at least some of these items have introduced dissonant notes for some listeners. The opportunity to achieve a successful isolation of the theme of the hour has been dissipated. Faced with a forced alternative, the minister has forfeited a useful isolation of his main theme by electing a self-defeating pursuit of promotion of many excellent matters among which he refused to make a choice.

3. *Learning is strengthened when the level of reward is high.*
People learn new responses under the incentive of increased
pay, enthusiastic compliments, desired recognition, coveted pro-
motions. In each case "reward has to be defined in terms of the
receiver." [10] What the receiver regards as most rewarding is the
crucial matter. Once this has been determined, and the reward
is suited to the receiver's needs or goals, the learning bond is
strengthened. In preaching, this indicates the importance of
selecting the theme and developing the message in such a manner as to make it rewarding to the listener in terms of *his* concerns and goals. The selection of novel themes and "catchy"
titles is not enough. Does the listener find healing where *he*
hurts? Does he see help on the problem that has been baffling
him? Can he feel, from the beginning of the message to its
close, the presence of something that advances him toward his
most meaningful objectives? Any sermon that meets these tests
will fulfill one of the prime needs of the learning situation. For
this reason, the Biblical sermon that uses Scripture interpretation
to interpret the listener's life and the sermon that functions as
"individual counseling on a group scale" go far toward meeting
the needs of good teaching.

4. *Reducing delay in reward to a minimal level strengthens
the stimulus-response bond and thus reinforces learning.* Many
rewards are necessarily delayed. The newspaper reader, for
example, receives delayed rewards when he reads news on public
affairs, social issues, the arts and sciences. But rewards are immediate, in terms of entertainment, as he reads sensational
stories, sports news, and the like. In the nature of the pulpit
message, it must deal with long-term goals and delayed rewards.
For this reason, the preacher needs, where honesty and spiritual
integrity permit, to relate remote rewards to some that are more
immediate. "We can often start with a penultimate question, and
then give the ultimate answer. Our problem is to help our
hearers see that the thing that is bothering them is really a
deeper question than they themselves realize and thus see that
the Christian answer is relevant and connected—and will take
them further even than they have wanted to go." [11]

5. *Responses that can be made with the least effort are most likely to be retained and thus to induce the desired learning or action.* On this principle, advertising appeals enclose a simplified reply form, together with a self-addressed, postage-paid envelope; or television commercials urge a telephone reply ("no need to write in") and give the telephone number repeatedly both vocally and in visual symbols. In preaching, this suggests the simplified response to the evangelistic altar call (with pre-announcement of all that will ensue). This also suggests the importance of classes and other support groups to reduce the stress of lone effort for those who have taken a message seriously and need help in following through on its implications.

6. *Images that find support in a coherent integration with other images are thereby strengthened as an aid in learning.* A good course or textbook necessarily treats numerous problems, sometimes of quite diverse kinds; its success depends on the skill with which these varied elements are fused into a coherent pattern whose parts mutually reinforce one another. For pulpit teaching this suggests the importance of some form of planning over an extended period. The course of sermons from a Bible book or a section of the church's lectionary offers one type of plan. Many able preachers build such segments into a preaching program for the year, with Scripture and theme scheduled for each Sunday.[12] In addition to the help it affords the preacher by providing a way of gathering material for themes in process of preparation and by allowing sermons to grow slowly into wholeness in the preacher's mind, planned pulpit teaching aids the coherence of images for the listener by (*a*) allowing ideas to reinforce one another as the year progresses, (*b*) providing balance in which the various aspects of the Christian message find a place without overstressing the preacher's enthusiasms or neglecting areas to which he is less sensitive, and (*c*) giving wholeness to the articulation of the faith.

A teaching pulpit that makes skilled use of these insights developed by psychologists and educators can assist the listener to become an active learner. So doing, it can win an eager hearing without resort to sensationalism or unworthy bids for popularity. Finding that the preacher is helping them to achieve their own most worthy goals, people will respond, and real growth will ensue.

Teaching Power in Liturgical Elements

The building of associations around liturgical materials often repeated in the life of the church can serve as a strong teaching method. Many vital theological materials find frequent restatement through worship in every congregation; the member who is helped to gather enlarged meanings around them matures in Christian understanding.

The Sacraments lend themselves to such interpretation. Baptism, for example, as the rite of entrance into the faith, conveys the gospel in microcosm: God's gracious acceptance into a fellowship no merit has earned; forgiveness and cleansing as entrance into a new life that calls for continued growth and confirmation; the death of an old self and the sharing in Christ's resurrection (Rom. 6:3–11). Communion, too, opens opportunities for theological teaching. The four central acts in which our Lord takes common things essential to our life, blesses them, breaks and divides them among us, and gives them back with new significance (Mark 14:22) typify his creative touch on our life. The respective sections of the Communion liturgy of any denomination can be examined and interpreted; each section shows forth with dramatic power an important aspect of the gospel.

Other recurring elements of liturgy lend themselves to teaching uses. (*a*) The Lord's Prayer can be given powerful associations by careful interpretation in a sermon or series of sermons. (*b*) The various creeds, historic and contemporary, used in the church's worship, condense the central doctrines. A series of sermons that explore these, one by one, to discover their meaning and their bearing on current ongoing affairs can help every future repetition of these affirmations to bring these functional centralities to mind in meaningful review. (*c*) The questions any denomination puts to new members received into its fellowship focus attention on what the denomination holds to be key ingredients of a growing Christian life. Luminous sermons interpreting these focal elements can make the periodic reception of members a reinforcing review of cardinal matters of faith at each subsequent hearing of the questions.

The Christian Year as a Teaching Guide

Celebration of the Christian year can focus upon basic elements of the gospel at their respective liturgical seasons. Theologically understood, the year is far more than a calendar device or an annual recapitulation of events in the life of Jesus. Season by season, it celebrates the structural elements in the message with which the church from its beginning, and continuing through the ages, has confronted the world.

Scholars such as C. H. Dodd have shown that the preaching of the apostles was not a subsequent outgrowth of the "simple story of Jesus" enshrined in the Gospels; the preaching antedated the Gospels and gave them their content and structure. According to Dodd's analysis, the preaching of Paul, as it can be reconstructed from sermons reported in the Acts and from Paul's own résumés scattered through his letters, builds upon a series of assertions of the good news.

"The prophecies are fulfilled, and the new Age is inaugurated
       by the coming of Christ.
He was born of the seed of David.
He died according to the Scriptures, to deliver us out of the
       present evil age.
He was buried.
He rose on the third day according to the Scriptures.

He is exalted at the right hand of God, as Son of God and
Lord of quick and dead.
He will come again as Judge and Saviour of men." [13]

Dodd notes that the Petrine form of this message did not greatly
differ from the Pauline, except for Peter's steady inclusion of
references to our Lord's life and ministry in contrast to Paul's
direct passage from the nativity to the crucifixion. Dodd adds
that the apostolic preaching always closed with an appeal to
repent and believe the gospel and thus to enter a new life.

This apostolic preaching, or *kērygma,* underlies the basic doctrines of Christianity and focuses the concerns of the successive
seasons of the Christian year. The parallels between *kērygma,*
creed, doctrine, and season are set forth in Table I.

At only a few points do these parallels require comment. (*a*)
The cohesiveness of history, which underlies the fulfillment of
prophecy and the inauguration of the new Age, roots in God's
acts and points to God the Father Almighty, who reigns in
history. This historic continuity is one important element of the
Advent message. Advent reappears in the *kērygma's* announcement that Christ will come again, the only element of the apostolic message that does not follow the unfolding year in chrono-
logical sequence. This announcement gives Advent its other
important themes: the eschatological hope and the message of
judgment. (*b*) Jesus' character, shown in his life and ministry,
reveals the character of the Father. Epiphany—the root meaning of the word being "manifestation"—is the appropriate season for emphasis on this revelatory element in the teaching. (*c*)
The call to repent and receive the new life never carries a New
Testament expectation that men can do this in their own
strength; it is a gift of the Holy Spirit. It thus opens the meaning
of the Pentecost season as a time for teaching on growth in the
new life through the power of the Spirit.

This analysis of the Christian year does not assume that the
specified doctrines can be preached only in the seasons for
which they supply the respective keynotes. Nor does it suggest

that nothing but these doctrines can be properly preached in the designated seasons. It does give a clue to the drama of the Christian year, however, with no little help in understanding the historic lectionaries. Followed by a preacher with creative imagination and sensitivity to the needs of his people and his time,

Table I. THE KĒRYGMA IN THE CHRISTIAN YEAR

Kērygma	Creed	Doctrine	Season
Prophecies fulfilled, new age begun in Christ	God the Father Almighty	God's reign in history	Advent
He was born of the seed of David	Jesus Christ his only Son, our Lord	Incarnation	Christmastide
Christ "went about doing good"		God's revelation in Christ	Epiphany
He died to deliver us out of the present evil age	Suffered . . . crucified . . . dead, buried	Reconciliation, expiation, atonement	Lent
He rose . . . the third day	The third day he rose	Resurrection	Eastertide
He is exalted as Lord	He ascended into heaven	Universal Lordship of Christ	Ascensiontide
He will come again as Judge and Savior	From thence he shall come to judge	Eschatological hope, judgment	Advent
Repent and receive the new life	The holy catholic church, communion of saints, forgiveness, resurrection, life everlasting	New life through the Holy Spirit	Pentecost

it can make of the yearly cycle a framework for significant teaching.

PROBES

1. Thor Hall, *The Future Shape of Preaching* (Fortress Press, 1971), is oriented to the preacher's role of theological teacher; see especially pp. 80–90. James S. Stewart, *A Faith to Proclaim* (Charles Scribner's Sons, 1953), sets forth central teachings of the *kērygma* as they are perceived by a great preacher-theologian. Merrill R. Abbey, *Living Doctrine in a Vital Pulpit* (Abingdon Press, 1964), studies preaching specifically in terms of its systematized teaching function.

2. One of the Probes in Chapter 7 suggested the planning of a course of sermons for one liturgical season. You might now coordinate with the course you planned then another course to be used in an adjacent liturgical season, to include (*a*) stated objectives you hope to achieve during the year; (*b*) a basic Scripture for each Sunday; and (*c*) a compactly stated theme for each Sunday, rooted in the chosen Scripture and aimed to meet a felt need of your people.

3. Basing your work on a doctrinal understanding of the seasons of the Christian year, as outlined in the closing section of this chapter, proceed season by season to incorporate the plans suggested above into a coherent teaching plan for a full year's preaching.

CHAPTER 9

Counseling from
a Pulpit Base

A minister who uniquely influenced religious thought and life in the first half of the twentieth century characterized preaching as "personal counseling on a group scale." [1] The image should not be pressed too far. The pulpit cannot provide the listener with opportunity to "talk out" his problem, a prime requisite of good counseling. Nor can the preacher maintain the wholly nondirective attitude inherent in some counseling strategies. Yet the analogy is suggestive. The sermon is most true to its intended function when it renders real help in meeting specific, identifiable needs. In his pulpit, the preacher supplies one side of a conversation that goes on continually in his pastoral dealings with his people, so that the effectiveness of his speaking stands in direct relation to the sensitivity of his hearing. Preaching thus becomes an integral part of the pastoral care of a parish.

Wherever a congregation assembles, whatever its size, the need for counsel is present. The pain of pervasive meaninglessness, endemic in technological society, confronts the preacher with the counselee's quest for meaning. The advertising slogans that identify merchandise ranging from cars to cosmetics as things "you can believe in" reveal the aching need to restore trust. Conflict and dilemma are universal in the human predicament. Domestic difficulties so constantly encroach upon homes that experienced counselors estimate that 33 percent of the families represented in any congregation will be facing serious adjustment problems.[2] No matter how urgent the social prophecy of the pulpit, the prophet dare not forget that he is also preaching to persons burdened with grief; many months after the death of his only son, a man long dedicated to the social thrust of the faith observed that, while he remained committed to his church's social relevance, he had become painfully aware of the all but complete silence of its pulpit on the aspects of the faith that deal healingly with death and grief. Where listeners hurt with such unmet needs, they are less able to hear other urgent messages.

The pastor who regularly faces the same congregation has both the opportunity and the responsibility for counseling from a pulpit base. It was once the fashion to speak of the "life-situation sermon" as one of the optional categories among which a preacher might choose. This segregating of sermon types is less useful than an understanding of the counseling relationship as a dimension of all preaching. The preacher becomes a counselor. He stands at the listener's side to help him find his way through the maze of difficulties that minister and parishioner share by reason of their common humanity.

Seeing a counseling dimension in *all* sermons does not lock the preacher into one unvaried pulpit pattern. He must continue to sound an evangelistic call, to explore the content of the faith as a teacher, and to confront with searching prophetic demand the evils and follies that ensnare men and society. As a pulpit counselor, however, he will do all this not as an oracle from without but as one who enters into the lives of others with a feeling for their personal needs and helps them find the solutions they are seeking. These solutions, he knows, must come from within the individuals who must ultimately take responsibility for carrying insight into action.

Preaching and Counseling Are Mutually Reinforcing

From a pulpit base, the minister can establish a relationship with persons that opens doors to counseling and makes fruitful pastoral care possible. Ministers who make counseling central in their ministry value the pulpit for this reason. A chaplain in a mental hospital, for example, regards his preaching as the most valuable single thing he does. The reason, he says, is not in prescriptions handed out in sermons, but in the identity he establishes in the pulpit. In that relation patients come to know him as a person and are later able to identify with him as a pastor.[3] Here they see him as one who cares deeply about persons, understands the depths of the human dilemma, and faces issues seriously but not judgmentally. In such a man they can confide.

Because preaching normally occurs within the setting of a worshiping congregation, it is strengthened by the power of a supportive group. Psychiatrists and social workers, recognizing the need for such support, are at pains to build group life for those whom they counsel. For the preacher who values the pulpit as a counseling resource, the congregation becomes such a group, already provided. Some pastors wisely draw persons with common problems together into support groups—couples with marital problems, or parents and teen-agers needing better relations. This adds a dimension to the therapeutic relation, but it occurs within the encompassing reality of the congregation.

It is sometimes objected that the preacher's functions, as moral conscience for society and as pastoral counselor for persons, work at cross purposes, so that if he fulfills one role he is thereby barred from the other. This can be a real danger for the preacher who is harsh, unsympathetic, or unskilled. If he sees all things in terms of "two-valued judgments"[4]—completely true, right, and good, or completely false, wrong, and evil—his rigid pronouncements necessarily isolate him from persons who most need help. But alternatively, without deserting his post in the Christian warfare against wrong and injustice, he may make himself more accessible to troubled people by his stance as one who knows the depth of the difficulty, but who also sees the complexities and knows his own involvement in the human predicament.

Reciprocal Functions of Pastor and Preacher

Pulpit preparation and pastoral care can be reciprocally enriching. In his study, preparing his sermons, the minister works also as a pastor whose people are with him in imaginary dialogue. He is diligent in his search for intellectual integrity and scholarly excellence, but he "does theology" less as an academic quest and more as a search for light on the shadowed places he has found in the troubled lives of his people.

When he leaves his study, the minister does not cease to be studious. As he goes about among his people, calling in their homes, visiting in the hospitals, following them to their places of employment, standing with them beside the open grave, counseling with them in their bewildered moments, he is no less their sympathetic friend for being also their theologian. Coming back from his rounds, he brings new problems to investigate theologically in his reflective hours of study.

In his pulpit he stands on a bridge between study and pastoral round. Here he speaks into the situations with which, throughout the week, he diligently counsels. His sermons cannot substitute for dealings with individuals, one by one, but his sermons can strengthen all that transpires in these relationships. In therapy for the grief-stricken, for example, both ministry within the congregation and one-to-one care are needed. Grief, in the bereaved, is more than a cataclysmic emotion; it is a separation anxiety[5] in which the loss of one who has become integral to the very existence of the mourner now calls that existence in question. With a part of himself gone—and that now seeming to be the most important part—the grief sufferer's identity is threatened. In confronting this crisis, both preaching and private counseling have their assigned functions.

The grief-sufferer needs to talk. The pastor is not alone in making that possible, but freeing the talk by his sensitive listening is a function he cannot shirk. Only by talking with one whose empathy releases him can the bereaved be freed from the anger and guilt that are components of grief. Only by talk can the sorrowing one reaffirm the good in himself that was represented by the deceased, the loss of which has threatened his own being. Only by talk can he resolve the conflict between the desire for, and the need to recognize and accept the loss of, the loved one. In such talk, he can begin to realize the resurrection of the deceased within his own ongoing life, pick up and renew significant relationships, and rediscover meaning in his life through renewal of his commitments. Adjustments at these depths are not achieved in passive receptivity. The pastor, or others who have learned to fulfill the pastoral role, must help to work them out in the give-and-take of personal conversation.

Yet preaching also plays its part. What the minister says in the pulpit can speak into the counseling conversation, aiding its advance. Sermons can help to interpret death and the separation anxiety of grief. Preaching can help those who have not yet experienced bereavement to think through some of its issues. Thus assisted in quiet times, they can come to a crisis in some measure prepared. As the sorrowing person and the more tranquil person face the processes of grief together within the supportive climate of the congregation, those who are crisis-threatened can be strengthened while others are awakened from escapism, sensitized, and forearmed. In all this the minister establishes a relation that aids present counseling and enhances his future usefulness when dark hours come.

What is true in the illustrative instance of grief is also applicable to most of the serious issues of life. Both the personal care of a concerned pastor and the pulpit guidance of a wise preacher are needed, and in the minister's day-to-day work the two functions reciprocally support each other.

Harry Emerson Fosdick: A Case Study

Counseling from a pulpit base was so much the heart of the ministry of Harry Emerson Fosdick that a careful examination of his preaching best illuminates its meaning and methods. In his vast Riverside parish, he might have been freed from the heavy demands of these personal contacts to give himself wholly to his distinguished preaching ministry. This temptation he resisted, however, making his work with individuals central.[6] As a result, his pulpit ministry was fed with an endless stream of insight, of which he said: "No matter how much a counselor may help his 'patients,' the chances are that they do as much for him as he does for them. If his sermons and books have point and relevance, if they strike home to vital problems and hit real nails on the head, the explanation lies in his clairvoyance, strenuously gained by sharing the struggles of human souls, one by one. At any rate, without the creative experience of personal counseling I never could have preached for twenty years in Riverside Church." [7]

Fosdick understood that "every sermon should have for its main business the head-on constructive meeting of some problem which was puzzling minds, burdening consciences, distracting lives." [8] Undertaking such a task, the sermon taps the springs of endlessly vital interest, for it falls into step with the listener's spontaneous concerns. In so doing, it enlists the hearer as a participant in the building of the thought. In one sermon, for example, Fosdick began, "One powerful influence in the life of all of us is the fact that our generation has lived through a long series of major disappointments." He enumerated World War I, the frustrated hopes of the World Court and the League of Nations, economic collapse, and the coming of World War II. To all this, he noted, the disappointments of "ordinary individual life" must be added, so that "a mood is created that none of us altogether escapes. It impinges like a climate on every one of us—call it by what special name you will—sadness, hopelessness, cynicism, disillusionment, moral apathy, lost faith in human possibilities." [9] In the ensuing quest for ways to keep open the road to the realization of those possibilities, the preacher was working at a task so obviously important to all who heard him that its success was as much their concern as his.

Preaching as Animated Conversation

Leafing through a volume of Fosdick's sermons is like over-hearing an extended conversation. In "What Does the Divinity of Jesus Mean?" he began: "This sermon springs from endless inquiries sent me by radio listeners. They want to know what the 'divinity' or 'deity' of Jesus means." After four intervening sentences Fosdick continued: "The reply to this question, if it is to be vital, must be personal. What does the divinity of Jesus mean to us in the actual practice of our daily lives?" [10] A little later, he picked up the question he heard people asking, "Where is God?" and said, "In response to that question some say we find God in the universe at large." Examining that, he concluded: "Well, I agree. But is that all? Others say we find God in the beauty of the world." Again he came fairly quickly to agreement, but pursued: "Is that all? Others say they find God in the moral order of the world." This, in its turn, he looked at sympathetically, agreed, and asked, "Is that all?" [11] This conversational dialectic led irresistibly to the acknowledgment that we find God most fully revealed in Christ.

The "If someone says, . . . I answer" device does not exhaust this strategy designed to dispel the image of "a preacher alone in the pulpit." The sense that "the people can be there too" is sustained in numerous other ways. Often the listener is directly addressed, in the second person of familiar conversation, never in accusation or complaint, but always in recognition of the situation or problem he shares with others. In nearly every sermon many questions are asked, and these are not rhetorical questions that have only one obvious answer. These are thoughtful questions that people are asking, questions that demand reflection, on which preacher and people ponder together. Again and again, strong objections to the sermon's thesis are taken into account, often beginning with the phrase, "Granted that . . . ," as if Fosdick were responding to a voice from the congregation. Having thus conceded points that seem fatal to the preacher's case, he then places them within a larger perspective, which diminishes their force.

Truth Serving a Purpose

In all this, Fosdick was not so much discursively exploring or actively debating an idea as he was moving toward the accomplishment of a purpose for and within persons. "A good sermon," he held, "is an engineering operation by which a chasm is bridged so that spiritual goods on one side—the 'unsearchable riches of Christ'—are actually transported into personal lives upon the other. . . . A lecture is chiefly concerned with a *subject* to be elucidated; a sermon is chiefly concerned with an *object* to be achieved." [12] This, of course, was not accomplished without important idea content, but the idea was always instrumental to the "object to be achieved" for persons. In his major study of Fosdick's preaching, Edmund Holt Linn refers to these two elements as the "specific purpose" and the "big truth." [13]

In one memorable sermon, for example, the "specific purpose" was to restore a sense of reality in prayer as a source of power for secularized men. "There are three ways in which men get what they want—thinking, working, praying," he began, noting that most people are agreed on the first two and doubtful about the third. After acknowledging some reasons why this is so, he turned to the "big truth": "Powerful personality is never created simply by thought and work. Powerful personality has deep interior resources of inspiration and intake. . . . Great living is not all output in creative thought and work; it is also intake." [14] All that happened in what followed advanced the march of that "big truth" toward the achievement of the "specific purpose."

For too long, preachers have discussed ideas, Fosdick contended, rather than creating experiences; but "a preacher's task is to create in his congregation the thing he is talking about." It is not enough to discuss repentance unless someone repents. Explanations of Christian faith are insufficient unless people go away more faithful. It will not do to "talk about the available power of God to bring victory over trouble and temptation" unless people are sent out "with victory in their possession." [15]

To achieve such availing participation in the lives of people, standing in their place, working with them on their problems, effecting changes, he maintained, requires "clairvoyance." [16] By this, of course, he did not mean occult extrasensory perception. Such penetration of another's situation grows out of pastoral concern and much deeply attentive sharing in the lives of others. The "clairvoyant" minister is he who continually goes where people are, opens himself to them, and lovingly shares their life. From this empathic sharing he returns to his study to make his frequently repeated analysis of his receiver-interactants, bringing their perplexity and need to focus in clear thought and deep feeling as he prepares to preach.

In all that he does, the counseling preacher maintains his stance as an interpreter of the Biblical message—or, as we have previously held, interprets the shadowed places in our tangled lives in the light of an understanding in depth of the Bible's insights. As Fosdick said of his own ministry, his emphasis on preaching as "personal counseling on a group scale" made the Bible more important, rather than less. Reared on the Scriptures and saturated with them, he declared, he "could not deal with any crucial problem in thought and life without seeing text after text lift up its hands begging to be used." [17] According to Linn's careful count, his sermons made, on the average, a dozen references to the Bible, sometimes in direct quotation, sometimes in indirect allusion.[18] In such preaching, Biblical interpretation comes alive through the hermeneutic that finds in Scripture compelling resources for understanding contemporary situations and winning victory over their perils.

Counseling from a pulpit base is thus seen not as a special kind of sermon added to other kinds. It is, rather, a total orientation of the preacher toward all that he does. In this orientation he brings the power of his pulpit to the assistance of his pastoral care of persons all through the week. By this orientation he takes up his position, not over against the listener as an advocate of an external cause or doctrine but beside him as a partner in matters that preacher and hearer seek to work out together. In the course of this orientation, the preacher best does his work as Bible interpreter, teacher, evangelist. He does not so much discuss psychology, or ethics, or sociology, or theology; he draws on the resources of these and all other disciplines in which he can gain skill, in order to deal with the real needs of persons and of the society of which he and they are constituent parts. Some methodologies are peculiarly adapted to this orientation. In this chapter we have reviewed a few of these methods; to others we shall give detailed attention in the remaining chapters of this book.

PROBES

1. The content of this chapter is helpfully supplemented by three books: Edgar Newman Jackson, *A Psychology for Preaching* (Channel Press, Inc., 1961); Charles F. Kemp, *Pastoral Preaching* (The Bethany Press, 1963); and Arthur L. Teikmanis, *Preaching and Pastoral Care* (Prentice-Hall, Inc., 1964). The work of Harry Emerson Fosdick so lights the way in this area that fuller study of him is of great worth. His autobiography, *The Living of These Days* (Harper & Row, Publishers, Inc., 1956), is a foundational document, and its fifth chapter contains his most extended discussion of preaching. *Riverside Sermons* (Harper & Brothers, 1958), constitutes the most representative anthology of his sermons. Edmund Holt Linn, *Preaching as Counseling: The Unique Method of Harry Emerson*

Fosdick (Judson Press, 1966), provides an admirable analytical study of Fosdick's communicative methods.

2. This would be a good time to prepare a sermon evoked by the "specific purpose" of meeting a need you have identified among your friends, classmates, or members of the congregation you know best. Make your perception of the need as sharp as you can by thinking concretely about individuals and the way this need manifests itself in things they have said or done. *Feel* the need yourself by putting yourself in their place. When you have thus identified your "specific purpose," make a careful study of a Biblical insight that speaks to it (applying methods learned—perhaps freshly reviewed—in Chapter 7). State this insight concisely in a sentence; this will be the sermon's "big truth." Now proceed to prepare the sermon in imaginary conversation with your people, bringing the "big truth" to bear, in as many ways as you can, upon the "specific purpose."

CHAPTER 10

Exploring Innovative Forms of Proclamation

Though innovative forms lend piquancy to proclamation, novelty is not their primary purpose. The electric media have created a new perceptual environment. By the time he is three years old, the average American child has spent more hours before the television screen than he will later spend in class in four years of college. "Television and stereo are the confirmation class par excellence for our adolescents in their rite of passage to moral maturity." [1] Amid such formative influences, new forms of proclamation are sought as attempts to gain clarity for those who hear and see in new ways.

The receiver and his environment change in other vital respects. Pluralism makes the impingement of cultures and subcultures omnipresent; innovative forms may aid in the communication of the message more convincingly to some of these culture groups. Innovations may advance communication between groups in Christian reconciliation. For such reasons as these, experimentation is needed.

This chapter does not attempt to crystallize new forms. To treat any of the experiments as completed models would be to defeat their purpose. Yet experimentation needs to proceed on the basis of examined principles, with some understanding of what other workers in the field have attempted. This chapter suggests some principles that may help to guide innovation, and points to typical forms on which experiments are under way. The concern is not with finished inventions but with continued exploration.

Context Shapes Perception

Six guideline principles merit consideration. The first reminds us: *Perception is shaped by context.* What we "see" is more than sensation; distance perception, for example, is less "seen" than interpreted. Shutting one eye at a time, one sees a slightly different scene from each eye's angle of vision; yet with both eyes open we do not see two scenes. The brain interprets the two raw sensations as a single entity as one learns to make judgments of depth and distance from these stereoscopic data.

Similarly, what have been called "optical illusions" are not really optical. Experiments at Dartmouth College demonstrate contextual influences on perception. In a laboratory room a girl in one far corner seems, from the viewer's vantage point, to tower hugely over the young man in the opposite corner. When the two change places, however, it is the young man who towers, and the girl becomes diminutive. This occurs because the mind of the viewer assumes that the room, which *appears* conventional enough, is rectangular as are all other rooms to which he is accustomed. This room, however, is so shaped that one far corner is much more remote than the other, and all else—including doors, windows, and the like—is scaled to support the impression of rectangular regularity. What the eye sees is a girl and a young man of similar height. What the mind interprets, on the basis of past experience and apparent data, is a vast discrepancy in size.[2]

This principle—perception shaped by context—demands attention in relation to preaching. Persons whose minds have been conditioned by the visual and acoustical context of the electric media perceive in ways altered by that experience. How can proclamation adapt presentation to the requirements of accurate and vivid perception in this new setting? Or in many

celebrative contexts created by contemporary worship? Amid
the varied life-styles represented in some congregations, what
forms of proclamation can be most persuasively understood? To
such questions a new generation of preachers must seek viable
answers.

Clarity Requires Redundancy

A second principle holds: *Redundancy is necessary for clarity.*
Language secures understanding by providing more than the
bare minimum of essential data. Consider, for example, that
"gospel in miniature," John 3:16. Reduced to "cablese," it
might read: "God loved gave Son whoever believes have life."
The basic elements are there, and even one not familiar with
the full text might puzzle them out. Clarity is advanced, however, if a few more elements are supplied: "God loved world
gave Son that whoever believes not perish have eternal life."
While that says it all, its clarity falls far short of the familiar
"God so loved the world that he gave his only Son, that whoever
believes in him should not perish but have eternal life." Between
bare cablese and full clarity there is a difference of fifteen words
and one punctuation mark. Biblical English is not decorative;
it does not embroider meaning with verbiage. Yet in this case it
arrives at full clarity by redundancy over minimum essentials in
the ratio of twenty-three words to eight.

We have seen some applications of the redundancy principle
to preaching, as in the numerous repetitions of theme in Harry
Emerson Fosdick's sermon "The Means Determine the End,"
or in the reduplication of communicative data through added
channels as part of the rationale of the mixed-media presentation. The principle may well guide experimentation with innovative forms. (*a*) The "cool media" style should not lead to
such low definition of the message as to endanger its clarity. (*b*)
Multiplying channels through additional media should be done,
not in faddish preoccupation with the media as ends, but in
careful attempt to reinforce clarity through redundancy.

Reality Limits Abstraction

A third principle warns: *Reality in communication requires reduction of the level of abstraction.* Generalizations need constant checking by cases. Language makes abstractions that range farther and farther from experienced cases. S. I. Hayakawa orders these in a "ladder" according to their distance from experienced reality. Beginning with the "cow known to science" as a peculiar arrangement of "atoms, electrons, etc.," he proceeds to successive levels of abstraction: the cow we perceive in the pasture; "Bessie," a name given to a particular cow; the concept "cow," covering creatures of its class; the word "livestock," used to include horses and pigs along with cows; the term "farm assets," enlarging the coverage to plows, harvesters, etc., along with cows and other livestock; the general concept, "assets," lumping the cow, "Bessie," and other farm assets into a package with bonds, bank accounts, town real estate, and the like; and finally the highest-level abstraction, "wealth," which could widen the scope of assets to include a happy family, human resources, and other intangibles.[3]

Educators as well as semanticists are concerned about abstractions. Edgar Dale constructs a pyramid that he calls the "cone of experience," with direct experiences, in which one must make decisions and assume responsibilities, as its base. Successive layers are, by increasing steps, removed from this direct experience: contrived experiences, dramatic participation, demonstrations (as in the laboratory), field trips, exhibits, motion pictures, radio, recordings, still pictures, visual symbols, and verbal symbols, in an ascending order of abstraction.[4] If one accepts the assumption that learning advances in proportion to involvement in real experience, this suggests that communication in ministry needs to seek ways to dip into the cone of experience as near to its base as circumstances permit.

The worth of abstractions is beyond question. One who never rose above the base of the cone of experience or the bottom rung of the ladder of abstraction could not organize his thinking. Without higher levels of abstractions, communication would be limited to pointing to objects and pantomiming actions. Apart from abstractions a cultural heritage could hardly be passed from generation to generation. Yet accurate communication depends on continuous movement up and down this scale. Particulars need to be gathered into abstractions, and abstractions kept accurate and vivid by reference to particulars. Whether in speaking and writing or in other media, much of the art of useful communication depends on alternation between the general and the particular.

This principle, important to all preaching, needs special emphasis when experimentation is under way. The experimenter needs to note both the advantages and the limitations of dramatization, the electric media, and the use of visual symbols. On the one hand, they are nearer than the spoken word to direct experience and can thus convey their message with power; on the other, they may so fix attention on the particular that the "portable" quality of the generalization is lost. Film, for example, easily portrays concrete experience, but the communication of intangibles through film is a demanding art. Yet it must not be forgotten that much of the best in the Christian message moves in the realm of the intangible.

Culture Calls for Empathy

A fourth principle states: *Communication that relates one to culture, his own or that of others, requires empathic experience.* Ross Snyder speaks of the universal need for "a lived answer to the question 'who and what and where is my people?' " [5] Central to finding one's identity is the experience of knowing some group as "my people." The discovery cannot be abstract; it must be a "lived experience." When, as in the Sacraments vividly celebrated, there is strong empathy with "my people" and their tradition, something saving has occurred.

But there is also need to transcend one's own culture enough to achieve communication with members of another. The question of cultural isolation and imperialism is raised by Snyder's emphasis as he writes: "Communal celebration is a mode of immersing ourselves in some culture. Saturating ourselves with it, soaking it up into our fiber. . . . Such culturing is the utmost essential of any celebration. Today we have to *create* culture. Not only each generation, but every week and every day." [6] The civilized mind, however, must transcend its own culture. Innovators who would "soak up" some prized culture or subculture must beware of the danger of missing empathic understanding of culture groups beyond their own. One of the rich contributions of the dramatic arts, music, and film is their ability to carry us into *other* men's "lived answer to the question 'who and what and where is my people?' " Experimenters with new forms may well utilize the opportunities afforded by contemporary media, both to identify themselves savingly with their own people and empathically to understand others.

Communication Needs Participation

A fifth principle, familiar in these pages, states: *Messages are communicated best among active participants.* The SMCR ("source-message-channel-receiver") model pointed to this principle as it studied the receiver as well as the source in terms of the same attributes—including knowledge, attitudes, and communication skills. The consideration of interaction as the essential factor in meaningful communication, the underscoring of the dialogical relation, and the stress on the need for feedback in opinion change, all explored this principle. One of the chief goals of experiments with new forms of proclamation should be the involvement of the receivers in communication in which they are active participants.

Symbols Need Long Growth

A sixth principle declares: *Symbols that carry authentic religious meaning are products of growth, not manufacture.* Paul

Tillich served as a spokesman for this truth. Religion, "what concerns us ultimately," he held, answers the question of the meaning of life, an answer conveyed by symbols, not signs. A true symbol is not a mere conventionalized code sign on which men have agreed but a powerful reality in itself, grown in the subconscious, not made.

Such symbols, Tillich taught, have a twofold effectiveness. (*a*) They "open" truth and meaning. They are revelatory, showing forth reality in a unique way; and they open something deep within us, relating some aspect of reality to something basic in ourselves. (*b*) They heal. Their saving power is seen in the way in which the cross conveys the therapy of forgiveness, beyond the capacity of conceptual formulas to match. It is seen in the way in which liturgical acts carry a cleansing sense of the presence of the Holy.

The power of such symbolization, according to Tillich, comes to us most fully in the four elements of a devotional act: (*a*) The self-giving of the Holy, as in the Sacraments; (*b*) the divine Presence perceived and received, as in prayer and contemplation; (*c*) some sacrifice in which we surrender ourselves to the Ultimate; and (*d*) symbols that carry the revealing and healing power of the divine Love.[7]

Experimentation with new forms needs to give careful consideration to this distinction between symbols grown in the subconscious and signs ingeniously manufactured. The once-popular vogue for adapting Communion elements, for instance, to changing group mores (as when "Coke" and potato chips were substituted for bread and wine!) may lose the power of symbols rooted in the subconscious by attempting to speak only in signs that have current relevance. It is the genius of the innovative form to be timely, and of the slowly grown symbols to be permanently powerful. Between the two there is inevitably tension, which should not be too lightly resolved. The price of authenticity is to live with the tension.

Some Experimental Sermon Models

One experimental sermon model uses visual, recorded, and dramatic media. The chancel drama or film that conveys the message of the hour has long been in occasional use. In a developing variant the sermon uses these media for brief introduction to the message, as insets within it, or as entities with which the preacher engages in dialogue.

In one sermon on this model the preacher engaged in exchange with the musical *Man of La Mancha,* based on Cervantes' classic, *Don Quixote.* The preacher began the story and, at intervals, played stereophonic records of some of its music. These insets supplied one side of a dialogue in which the sermon replied to the lyrics, finally drawing the congregation into a share in the response.[8]

In another adaptation, the sermon began with the ten-minute film, *Very Nice, Very Nice,* a chilling collage dealing with modern society and its wars. This was followed by a short exposition of I Thess. 5:1–11, with its depiction of dark crisis times and its reassuring challenge: "But you are not in darkness, brethren, for that day to surprise you like a thief. For you are all sons of light and sons of the day." [9] The congregation was divided into buzz groups to share its thought on the film and Scripture exposition. Two or three of the groups were asked to report, and the minister closed with a brief challenge.[10] This is one of numerous uses that might be made of the single-concept film, which in ten minutes or less enables an audience to share a poignant experience, empathize with a character, or get hold of an idea in terms of the feelings it generates. Similar use might be made of drama, original or drawn from a longer play, enacted by members of the congregation.

The expectations-response model builds on the theory that learning is accelerated when the student's expectations are identified in advance and taken into account in the teacher's presentation. This model proposes a three-step procedure. (*a*) The preacher announces, a week in advance, the objectives he hopes to achieve through his next sermon, keeping the focus on intended outcomes, rather than theme or text. (b) Early in the service in which the sermon is preached, the people are asked to write on cards the personal expectations that have been awakened in them, and these are collected and given to the minister, who has opportunity for at least hasty review of them before preaching his sermon. (c) After the sermon, which the minister has attempted to adapt to the needs reflected on the cards, the people are asked to write on a second card the degree to which their expectations have been fulfilled.[11] This model tends to make listening more purposeful, gives the advantages of evaluative response after the sermon, and provides helpful feedback for the preacher's subsequent attempts. The brevity of the time allowed for the minister to absorb the expectations and adapt his presentation to them would seem to be a major handicap, but this difficulty could be met by collecting the cards through the mail or on the previous Sunday.

Several varieties of experiment can be grouped under the heading of the dialogue model. The talkback forum and feedback team discussed in Chapter 6 are among its applications. In an interesting variant of the talkback forum, Ross Snyder proposes that the people be given magazines and newspapers from which to cut designs, pictures, words, colors, to be pasted together into a collage representing responses awakened by the sermon. They are thus involved in ways not merely verbal. If there is opportunity for exchange of views and feelings regarding the collages, worship and learning may be augmented. For the small congregation, or for a class or other group which might undertake it after the service, this can lead to creative and moving experiences.

In another variation of the talkback forum, the minister preaches his sermon in segments, each of which is followed by a response from a representative of some identifiable part of the congregation. On one occasion an older member, a young adult, and a youth might respond; on another, a black person, a white, and a member of some other ethnic group.[12] Numerous additional categories can be devised. Developing in this fashion, the sermon partakes of the nature of both unfolding dialogue and talkback forum.

Some experiments have initiated dialogue between the preacher and the whole congregation. The minister introduces a theme or exposition on a text. The congregation is then invited to contribute reflections and experiences, raise questions, suggest implications. For this purpose they may remain in one large body or divide into small groups of six or eight persons.[13] The formlessness of this type of dialogue can be a source of freshness, but it also exposes this procedure to the risks of unplanned impromptu discourse.

In other dialogues two ministers, either from the same staff or from neighboring churches, develop a theme together; or a minister and a lay person or youth share the exchange. The dialogue may take on an ecumenical coloration as members of different faiths share a message, examining what is distinctive in each and what they have in common. Dialogue may approach the theme in mutual support, by question and answer, or in the frank statement of conflicting views that clarifies issues but holds them within the embrace of the community of faith.[14]

Useful dialogue requires careful preparation. Delivery from manuscript risks loss of the spontaneity that is the genius of this type of discourse; but, at the other extreme, the occasional dialogue sermon attempted by participants who agree on a general theme and depend on the charm of novelty to carry an otherwise unprepared conversation, invites the self-defeat that usually attends carelessness in great matters. There needs to be careful definition and narrowing of the subject, much previous thought and study devoted to the matters under discussion, thorough acquaintance by each participant with his partner's point of view, and an agreed outline of the objectives and content of the dialogue.

Among those who have worked with the dialogue model an emerging consensus underscores its values. It has inherent fac-

tors of interest because of its built-in drama. Its dialectics involve the congregation in working out ideas. It sharpens issues
in the give-and-take of discussion that can present two or more
sides through the testimony of convinced advocates. It makes
unwelcome ideas more difficult to tune out, as they are expressed
by neighbors or fellow worshipers. It gives lay participants the
learning experience, long enjoyed by ministers, of preparing
their thought on significant questions for articulate expression.
And in its involvement of many persons in the preaching, it
employs a *method* congruous with the *message* of God's near-
ness in the common life.[15]

Whatever the model used, if the presentation is to achieve
depth and worth, it will require certain constant factors essential to all useful discourse, whether traditional or innovative: a
sharply defined idea, an articulate communicative design, factors that evoke interactive interest, vital substance to communicate, integrity of style, and authenticity in the communicator himself. To these factors the remaining chapters of this book
are directed.

PROBES

1. No extensive literature on experimental forms of preach-
ing has yet developed. William D. Thompson and Gordon C.
Bennett, *Dialogue Preaching: The Shared Sermon* (Judson
Press, 1969), contains much practical help.

2. Write a brief critique of one or more of the guideline
principles suggested in this chapter. On the basis of such thinking, share with others a discussion seeking to evaluate these
principles and work out their implications. Can you devise other
guidelines to direct innovation?

3. Using one of the models suggested in this chapter, prepare
and present a sermon to your class or some other congregation.
Evaluate the effectiveness of your presentation in the light of
the guideline principles.

CHAPTER 11

Releasing the Dynamics of the Idea

How does preparation of a useful sermon get started? Where do productive ideas come from? How can one maintain a dependable flow of creative ideas, week in and week out across the years? In seeking cumulative power by scheduling themes in a long-time plan, what source can one rely on for a stock of germinal ideas? Questions such as these confront beginner and veteran alike. No flight from traditional to innovative forms escapes them. Releasing the dynamics of a strong idea can point the way to form, but an ingenious form with vague content can produce only froth.

Our earlier examination of the SMCR model revealed three dimensions of any message: content, treatment, and code. *Content* is the basic idea, the answer to the question: Stripped of all its rhetorical flourishes, what does the message really *say*? What core meaning makes a difference? *Treatment* is the name we give to the arrangement and order in the message. What comes after what? How does the design unfold? How does the outline hold together? *Code* is our designation for the symbols and signs used to convey the message. At what language level does it move? What figures of speech, illustrations, redundancies, and supportive media body it forth? Content, treatment, code—these, we have seen, are the constituent elements of any message. Because treatment and code are most apparent, we are often tempted to invest our major time and attention in them, hastily assuming that we have the content, the dynamic idea, sufficiently in mind.

For this reason, the novice often complains that, despite the promising material he has brought together, he can't get the sermon to "jell." Or the more experienced preacher brings off a lively, sometimes "inspiring" rhetorical feat, though his more discerning listeners know, and his own conscience may tell him, that not very much has been said. If preaching is to be true to its commission, altering opinions, changing lives, interpreting our existence, providing continuing education in doctrines that evaluate conduct and guide affairs, counseling troubled people at the points of their perplexity and need, lively elements of code and treatment are not enough; only potent content, a well-wrought central idea, will do.

Marks of a Valid Idea

In five succinct statements, H. Grady Davis sets boundaries within which one may recognize a valid sermon idea.[1] They afford useful guides and discerning tests for our work. Of the idea, Davis says:

1. "It must be narrow enough to be sharp." Does it include too much? Faith, for example, is the key to salvation, but to say "Faith" is not to state an adequate sermon subject. It is too broad, too ill defined. It needs narrowing. "Faith as the empowering source of good works"; "Faith as the key to meaning in life's ambiguities"; "How to maintain faith in a world of contradictions"—these are statements of themes that could germinate into useful sermons. But "Faith" is a subject without a predicate; it needs to be narrowed.

2. "It must have in it a force that is expanding." Narrowing must not leave it inert. There must be important things to be said about it: a series of declarations showing vital things it means, or a series of significant reasons why it is true in spite of appearances to the contrary, or a series of implications that follow from it. Something in it must cry out to expand.

3. "It must be true." This should go without saying, but sometimes our haste to get on with the development of an attractive conception leads us to neglect adequate testing of its truth. How deeply do we ourselves believe it? How has it been productive in our own lives? If we have neglected it or been unfaithful to it, what was the cost? Until we know the idea to be true in ways that matter decisively to us, it is not ready to play its productive part in creating a valid sermon.

4. "It must be loaded with the realities of the human heart." Its truth must be more than academic. It must rise out of the joys and agonies of existence. It must meet men and women where they live, must be able to enter meaningfully into their lives of burdensome humdrum and demanding crisis.

5. "It must be one of the many facets of the gospel of Christ." It is not everyday wisdom gained mainly from other sources; it is not law alone—all advice, urgings, and exhortations; it must carry the good news of God in Jesus Christ. This does not exclude surgery on the moral conscience. This does not bypass ills of the common life. But *the valid sermon idea must bring some aspect of the good news to bear upon some clearly discerned sore spot* in the affairs of individuals or of society.

How does a working minister go about releasing such dynamics to give a dependable flow of valid ideas?

Thought Is Dialectic

The best ideas arise out of dialogue. A question is asked, and one begins to search for an adequate answer. As Chapter 9 noted, one of Harry Emerson Fosdick's sermons arose from a question asked in many letters from his radio audience, "What does the divinity of Jesus mean?" Another vigorous preacher, James Armstrong, devised an influential sermon as an attempt to answer the question many people were asking, "How bridge the generation gap?" [2]

The dialogue may be internal, the minister posing questions to himself. In the midst of our pervasive escapism, he may ask, how can people be prepared to meet death victoriously? When

many leaders were bewailing the divisions within the body of
Christ, Eugene Carson Blake put to himself the question, What,
specifically, can we *do* to help the church move toward unity?
The sermon that launched the Consultation on Church Union
was the result.[3]

Internal dialogue may arise from the clash of events. Ernest
T. Campbell observed the injustices and absurdities that seem
to be embedded in our existence, and their collision with our
notions of a kindly Providence. "How do we know that there
is any discrimination at all within God concerning good and
evil?" he asked. "How can we be sure that ambiguity is not
the beginning and the end as well as the middle of things?" [4]
Bringing the clash and its question into confrontation with Jesus'
assurance that God "makes his sun rise on the evil and on the
good, and sends rain on the just and on the unjust" (Matt.
5:45), he produced a helpful sermon.

Dialogue may express agreement as well as tension. Elements
in the minister's reading or experience may coalesce into a compelling idea. Donald M. Baillie found such fusion between a
Robert Louis Stevenson story and a Pauline saying. In the story,
two men notice a diving costume on the seashore and fall to
speculating about it. "It comes up out of the sea, dripping with
water, and goes down again, and comes up again dripping with
water, and all the while the man inside is untouched—as dry
as if he had remained on land." [5] One man wondered if there
might be something one could wear that would allow him to
move through the world, with all its pain and disturbance, and
remain similarly unscathed. To that, the other replied, "Yes, it
is called self-conceit." Whereupon his companion asked, "Why
not call it the grace of God?" Baillie took note of these two
kinds of armor used by different men, hearing Paul enter the
discussion with his words "not I, but the grace of God which
was with me" (I Cor. 15:10, KJV). From this fusion of story
and text grew the idea of his sermon on "Pride and the Grace
of God."

Productive thinking inevitably takes this dialectic cast. A question seeks an answer; an assertion meets a contradiction, leading to a quest for resolution; a truth, sensed dimly at one point, grows in strength as it finds corroboration at another. As we noted in our study of Fosdick's preaching, the dialectic joining of a "specific purpose" to deal helpfully with a perceived need, together with a "big truth" rooted in a Biblical insight, produced the nucleus of his typical sermon. Germinal ideas release their dynamic in such give-and-take.

The Sermon Idea as an Ellipse

To employ a geometric analogy, we can say that for the Christian interpreter the dialogue takes the form of an ellipse, with one focus in the text and the other in a clearly perceived human situation. John Knox gave this truth its classic expression: "The preacher is not repeating, over and over again, an ancient chronicle; he is bearing witness to the quality and significance of a new communal life in which God is making available to us a new health and salvation. His preaching is an ellipse moving about the two foci of the ancient event and the always new life of the Spirit. . . . To hold the two elements together in their full integrity and distinctive force, *but to hold them together,* is the basic problem of preaching." [6] To handle the problem well, the preacher must deal with it from the moment of inception of the creative idea.

Saying about a text all the wise and illuminating things that the time will permit does not make a sermon. The text needs to be luminously studied and used, but such a circle around its single center is *commentary,* not preaching. Saying all the practical and helpful things about a troubled human situation that one can cram into the time is not a real sermon either. Light needs to fall on shadowed spots in our life, but such a circle drawn around our situation as a single center is *lecture,* not preaching. Only when both text and situation become formative foci does a valid preaching idea come to birth.

It is for reasons specifically theological that the dialectic which produces a preaching idea must be worked out around exactly *these* two elements. For the preacher must take both the Bible and troubled life seriously: the Bible as the normative center of his faith, troubled life as that which he and his message are sent to save. He cannot interpret the Bible faithfully without relating it to life. Every valid text arose out of a human situation and can be understood only in relation to that situation. But there can be no deep understanding of the Biblical situation until we are able to enter into it and feel it on our own pulse through its analogy to the situation in which we stand. In the light of Biblical insights we see what our life means.

The idea arises on the axis between the foci of text and human situation. The text confronts the situation with challenge or enters some troubled area with help. Our life puts questions to the text: how can we believe its affirmation, which much in our experience contradicts? The preacher takes his stance on the text-situation axis, seeking to bring to clear, concise statement some aspect of this dynamic tension. Truly understood and sharply stated, it can produce a useful sermon.

The human situation may find voice in what, in earlier chapters, we have called contemporary axioms. Emil Brunner once formulated a set of axioms which, he believed, underlay the secular life of the time,[7] some of which may serve to illustrate the text-situation axis. "What can't be proved can't be believed," one of them asserts. Biblical insight challenges that: "*Faith gives substance to our hopes, and makes us certain of realities we do not see*" (Heb. 11:1, NEB; italics added). Is there a sense in which both are true? When the chips are down, which can we live by? Somewhere on the axis of this confrontation there is a sermon needing to be preached.

An everyday axiom holds that "laws of nature determine everything," but the New Testament replies that "the law of the Spirit of life in Christ Jesus has set me free from the law of sin and death" (Rom. 8:2). As sons and daughters of a scientific age, we cannot forsake the laws of nature; but as disciples of a great Lord, we have a life-and-death allegiance to "the law of the Spirit of life in Christ Jesus." How can we resolve the tension between the claims? How can we relate the one law to the other in healthy living and social usefulness? Since science has passed from the "natural law" of closed systems to a realization that laws can be *used* to change life, the crucial question has become, What kind of men do the using? To this question, the law of the Spirit of life in Christ Jesus holds the answer.[8] In such ways as these the foci of text and situation generate the ellipse of the sermon idea.

Relating Text and Situation

The quest of the sermon idea may originate at either one of its two foci, but the quest does not issue in discovery until the other focus is found and the two foci are brought into relation with each other.

Pastoral concern may fix attention on the current needs of people in the parish. Dealing with a troubled parishioner, for example, the minister discovers an unexpungeable sense of guilt in which assurances of forgiveness repeatedly lead to new searches for sins in the more remote past. He knows something of the psychological dimension that must be dealt with; but is there not also a religious dimension? Beginning with this need, he delves more deeply in the gospel message to find the other focus of what becomes a helpful preaching ellipse.

On other occasions, a more general malaise drives him to a pastoral search for resources. He is troubled by the apathy and bewilderment settling on society, including his own people, under the too-long-sustained overstimulation produced by rapid technological and social changes. Or he sees widespread loss of morale in the wake of war that cannot be won, tolerated, or concluded. These and numerous other pastoral questions, initiated at the human-situation focus, send him to the Biblical focus in the attempt to close the ellipse.

Text and Situation ideas may begin to form alternatively in the minister's hours of systematic Bible study. In these hours he is not consciously stalking sermons; he is deepening his knowledge of Scripture because it is important in its own right. Next year he will preach from the book of the Bible he is presently studying; now, however, he is searching the book for its own message. Or perhaps he is working his way carefully through the lessons in the lectionary for a season months in the future. As he delves in these passages, his hermeneutic studies keep him asking, What is the valid parallel situation today, through which I can understand this message, and to which it speaks? Many of these studies thus lead him to a new understanding of the milieu that he and his people share. The Biblical focus finds the situation focus, closing the ellipse.

Refining the Idea: The Worksheet

A worksheet process is useful in refining the idea. An old maxim of public address advises:

> Write yourself empty,
> Read yourself full,
> Think yourself clear,
> Then compose.

The first clause is important. The speaker or preacher is greatly helped by getting everything he knows, thinks, or can imagine, concerning his subject, out before him. At this stage he is not writing the speech or sermon, and any struggle for order in his thought is premature. He is, rather, mining his interior resources for all available supplies that might conceivably be refined into usable form. Sometimes this is done by free association, one recollection leading to another. For many preachers, a series of operations suggested by a worksheet provides an aid in "writing themselves empty." Step by step, it clarifies and refines the idea.

Of seven single words that form the worksheet headings, the first is *Diagnosis*. Under this word the preacher writes the names or initials of at least a dozen persons with whom in the past week he has shared contacts through which he became aware of personal needs. He may also set down axioms he has derived from his study of the mass media, or other data drawn from his continuous audience analysis. No generalized data, however, can displace the need for a conscious awareness of individual persons and their concrete, current needs. These persons constitute a representative sample of next Sunday's congregation. All that happens in sermon preparation must be a deliberate attempt to communicate with them.

He next writes the heading *Prescription*. With the list of persons vividly before him, he imagines a group counseling session. If he could have an hour in such a circle, what insight would he hope each person could carry away? Inevitably the theme of the sermon under consideration exercises its gravitational pull on his thought, but at this point he does not try to formulate "answers" in terms of the selected theme. He asks, more broadly, What resource of the Christian gospel and fellowship can be helpful in each of these needs? As best he can, he records these insights.

Progressing to his third heading, he writes *Exposition*. In scheduling this sermon, he has previously studied the Bible passage that supplies the Biblical focus of the ellipse. Now, however, he returns to the study, this time in the light of the needs freshly visualized in the first two worksheet steps, putting the text under examination through the eyes of the persons he has listed. What questions would they ask about this text? At what points would they be incredulous? In what ways would it take on new color in speaking to them in their need? These reflections he enters under Exposition.

His fourth heading is *Experience*. Here he grows introspective, asking: How real is this idea to me? Do I fully believe it? What in my recent behavior verifies my belief? Have I sinned against it? When? How? At what cost? Has it in any way changed my life? This is his weekly confessional before God, induced by the message he is about to preach. Sometimes a portion of the data he records in this self-searching may provide a moving moment in the sermon. Whether he speaks directly of it or not, he will preach with greater reality for having thus delved in the personal dimension of his theme.

Under his fifth heading, *Program,* he writes a brief answer to the question, What ought to happen if people are convinced by this sermon? If someone came to me after I had preached, saying, "Your message is true, and I believe it. What should I do now?" what could I say in response? Better still, is there some suggestion of next steps that could become integral to the sermon? Not every sermon can or should be a "How to do it" exercise, but people have a right to expect some "handles" by which to grip the truth and put it to work. What practical "handles" can this sermon offer?

With his sixth heading, the minister moves to matters more technically rhetorical, as he writes the word *Purpose.* Although traditional rhetorical classifications of purpose—to entertain, to inform, to convince, to inspire, to move to action—are now seen to have limited usefulness, they retain practical descriptiveness. They can help the preacher "close in on" his idea.

For the pulpit, the first category of purpose—to entertain—is eliminated. The preacher's purpose is not to entertain. He has a responsibility to be interesting; to make the gospel dull is a travesty. If he is not able to awaken and hold interest, nothing else he attempts can reach its mark. Entertainment, however, can have no standing as a pulpit purpose.

Four categories remain, and among them the preacher must make a choice freshly adapted to every sermon. To inform is not his ultimate goal—he is seeking higher stakes in changed lives—yet, on occasion, information may provide the principal avenue to that goal. People need fuller understanding of the good news as a given text proclaims it; or they need to see the meaning of a dangerous path of conduct as an aspect of the Biblical message lights it up; or they need to know the meaning and practical implications of a neglected doctrine.

On another occasion the minister may decide that his purpose should be to convince. The people he seeks to reach are not so much endangered by lack of information as by lack of belief.

Their serious, perhaps not unreasonable, doubts bar access to important resources they need to live by. This sermon, he decides, must reach the goal of fuller life over the avenue of reinforced belief.

Another time, the purpose may be to inspire. The people this sermon ought to help, the minister says, are intellectually convinced of truths that do not touch their mainsprings of motive. They can confess the faith with the theologians, but they are not moved with the prophets and saints. To make the gospel's resources available for their need, this sermon should add to clarity of information and convinced belief an important dimension of inspiring motive.

For some sermons the purpose will be to move to action. This may need to gather up several of the other purposes within its scope, but the sermon will not have achieved its objective unless some people are moved to specific acts. In the stresses of a crowded life, they need to begin to release the springs of power found in definite, daily acts of prayer. Or in the material preoccupations of a secularistic orientation, they need to begin to hallow all of life by specific disciplines of stewardship. Or in the crisis of "spaceship earth," they need to express their care for God's creation by sharing in particular ecological reforms. Or as ghettos grow under the pressure of crowding, they need to support known housing patterns that open residential neighborhoods on an interracial basis.

Having determined which of these purposes has priority, and having written a statement of purpose as clearly and concretely as he can, the minister sets down his seventh heading, *Proposition*. Here he writes one all-important sentence that can be formulated with fullest clarity against the background of the foregoing process. This sentence states the affirmation which every part of the sermon will attempt to explain, support, or apply. In our study of the typical Fosdick sermon we spoke of the "specific purpose" and the "big truth." In the worksheet, the proposition concisely states the "big truth." If the minister's purpose is to inform, the proposition summarizes the essential truth to be conveyed; if to convince, it states what listeners are called to believe; if to inspire, it shows the thrust of the motivating reality; if to move to action, it states the act and its meaning in our life. All this is put in single-sentence form in order to assure unity in the sermon. If the sermon projects one unified idea, it should be possible to state this idea in one direct declarative sentence. If more sentences are required, the preacher knows that he has not yet sufficiently clarified his idea to release its dynamics, and he must return to his labor.

With the worksheet done, the preacher has determined his sermon's content and is ready to advance to treatment and code. This further work begins with the devising of a communicative design. Chapter 12 will provide help with that important step.

PROBES

1. H. Grady Davis, *Design for Preaching* (Muhlenberg Press, 1958), one of the strongest textbooks on preaching published in several generations, makes a key contribution in its treatment of the germinal idea of the sermon; see especially, Chs. 3, 4, and 5. John Knox, *The Integrity of Preaching* (Abingdon Press, 1957), contains, in fewer than one hundred pages, wisdom worthy of careful attention.

2. At a number of points in this chapter, illustrative material suggests the beginnings of a sermon idea, as in a stated axiom or pastoral problem. Select one of these, relate it to an appropriate Bible passage, and work out a statement of a sermon idea around the two foci thus envisioned.

3. Refine the idea you have stated for Probe 2, by carrying through the worksheet steps proposed in this chapter, visualizing a congregation of your friends or classmates, or some other congregation you know intimately.

CHAPTER 12

Creating a Communicative Design

From his work with the creative idea that determines a sermon's content, the preacher turns to the question of design. A strong handling of this question will simplify and strengthen all his remaining preparation, for a sound outline is a tool of orderly thought. It may break an idea into its constituent parts and reveal its meaning, structure a series of arguments to support a conclusion, or probe successive implications to show where a truth leads. A well-wrought outline guides the developing thought, holds the preacher to his subject, assures balance in presentation, and keeps the message moving. Good design thus contributes to the preacher's efficiency as a sound and orderly thinker.

Not the preacher, however, but the hearer focuses the interest of this chapter. What happens when people listen well? If they are to understand, remember, and act upon a message, to what questions must they find answers? In what sequence can the answers be most helpful? How can a sermon's design most directly provide for these listener needs? Our concern with design is not mainly esthetic. It is functional, not formal—a quest for the most efficient way to reach valid communication goals.

Questions That Guide Good Listening

To make sense of anything addressed to us, we must probe certain key queries: What is this speaker really talking about? What points is he making about it? In terms of my experience what does it mean? Do I believe it to be true? Does it make any difference that matters? [1] Good design "homes in" on these key quests with minimum delay. As near the beginning as possible it states the main idea. With unmistakable signposts it marks the principal points. Expeditiously it translates exposition into experience. Since impressiveness hinges on importance, it brooks no delay in verifying the value of its proposition.

What is the real subject? the listener must ask. This is not the same as asking the title (which may or may not tell much about the content of the message) or the text (since from the same text endless numbers of widely varied sermons have been preached). Before the listener can play his cooperative role in communication, he must identify the main idea, and the design that gets the idea clearly and forcefully stated with the least delay is generally the best.

A good listener is alert, next, to discover the principal supporting ideas and the way they are related to the main idea; and a good sermon design is structured to make these supporting ideas and relationships stand out so forcefully that they help a whole congregation to be good listeners. In false fear of becoming pedantic, speakers sometimes labor to cover over these structural matters; the result, which may satisfy the speaker's sense of beauty and polish, is the needless complication of the listener's task of getting answers to his cardinal questions.

As early as possible, the listener needs to answer the question, What purpose will this message help me to fulfill? Research data indicates that "if at the outset of the listening experience the auditor has clearly in mind the particular use he can make of the informative content of the message, he can increase the relevant comprehension-recall by a sizeable factor." [2] Students who know they are to be examined on a lecture or demonstration, for instance, and who know what knowledge is to be required of them, get far more from the experience than do those whose listening is not thus functionally oriented. Similarly, a sermon design which at the outset shows a significant purpose it is aimed to help people achieve will aid their listening to become purposeful and efficient.

Good listeners ask, How does this message relate to my experience? New material is best understood when it makes connections with what we already know, and the best designs are those which provide ample opportunity for listeners to set the main idea in meaningful contexts of familiar experience.

Listeners who know early what is being asked of them are best prepared to make favorable response. The surprise technique, in which the real demand or effective thrust of a sermon emerges unexpectedly in the closing moments, has a sometimes pleasantly spicy quality; but it allows too little time for the mind to respond on any important matter. The speaker who seriously asks a vital response needs to show early what belief or action he seeks and needs to design his message to bring its influence to bear to that end.

What is the real subject? What key ideas support the proposition? What purpose will this message help me to fulfill? How does the message relate to my experience? What appropriate response does this message ask? These questions, essential to good listening, can guide the preacher to communicative design. Generally that design is best which supplies these needs with the most dispatch.

Principles That Serve Understanding

Five principles of design guide the preacher to this goal.[3] The first deals with *unity:* a sermon is tied together into unified impact when *each major point is a supporting structure for the main proposition.* The points may tell what the proposition means, how it applies, why it is true, what it accomplishes. In a sermon intended to provide spiritual therapy for cold war tensions in the 1960's, for instance, J. Wallace Hamilton stated his main idea in the form of a contrast: "Because . . . fear is foremost in our thoughts, the major concern of America is how we can defend ourselves against . . . what communism is doing *to* us. . . . I am convinced that if we let it, communism can do momentous things *for* us." [4] The sermon then unfolded around subpropositions of that main proposition, each introducing a major section. "For one thing," Hamilton began, "communism is providing us with a *model* in which we can vividly see the alternative to Christian civilization." [5] Having discussed that, he continued, "Second, communism also provides us with a mirror in which we can see ourselves and our defections from the lifegiving faith." [6] When he had developed that point, he concluded, "Finally, communism is providing us with a motive, a rousing challenge, and a new incentive to Christian witness." [7] These three supporting structures of the main proposition built into the sermon a strong unity of impact.

The second principle deals with *order:* a sermon facilitates orderly thought when *the major steps in its design are of equal importance.* Because the thoughtful listener expects such orderly balance in a message on important matters, a point which towers over the others—or seems trivial by comparison—tends to skew his perception and make accurate understanding of the preacher's intent difficult.

The third principle deals with *movement: major points should not overlap.* Each should carry the thought forward by saying something clearly distinguishable from what has gone before. Order and movement are exemplified in the design of a sermon by James S. Stewart on I Kings 8:17–19. He began: "One major fact of life which we all have to meet is the experience of frustration. How to deal with frustration, how to manage it in a truly Christian way—this is one of life's critical tests." From that brief but effective introduction he moved directly to the development of a design whose key statements were: "Consider, first, the varied forms frustration takes. . . . Let us pass on, in the second place, to consider the Bible and frustration. . . . This brings us to our third point: the divine adjudication of frustration. . . . Notice, finally, the triumph over frustration." [8] Points clearly distinguishable and of equal or comparable importance gave this sermon its vital sense of order and movement.

The fourth principle deals with *proportion: the major points should be stated in parallel construction.* This helps the listener to identify the key statements. The unskilled speaker may state one point as a *topic* to be discussed, another as a *question,* another as an *assertion,* and perhaps a final one as an *exhortation.* He has thus deprived the listener of the helpful cues that could have come with parallel statement in the same grammatical construction: all questions, or all assertions, or whatever the case might be. In the examples we have noted, Hamilton's main points were all stated as declarative sentences of affirmation; Stewart's were all topics to be discussed. David H. C. Read designed a helpful sermon on Acts 17:21 around questions. The rather long introduction began with a question, "Do you like change—or do you distrust it?" [9] This extended opening led up to the key statement of the main idea: "We feel the need to re-examine the things we have professed to believe, to get out of the rut, to brace ourselves for changes—even painful changes—in our religious ideas and practices." [10] The two major sections of the sermon then treated that idea in the light of the questions: "Do we need a new religion?" [11] and "Have you really tried the one you were given?" [12] Three questions, to open the introduction and the two main sections, gave the sermon its helpful sense of proportion.

The fifth principle deals with *climax: points should be arranged in an ascending scale of impact.* We need to distinguish between two sequential orders present in any discourse: the *conceptual* and the *affective.* To begin at a high pitch of emotional impact and allow the feeling tone to decline in subsequent points would be so obviously anticlimactic as to invite disaster. Emotional climax is a clear necessity in holding listener attention and interest.

It is not so clear that an ascending scale of *conceptual* importance is a mark of good design. The strongest ideas may be best dealt with early in a sermon or address, while the minds of listeners are fresh and before fatigue effects have set in. Some research data indicates, though without full conclusiveness, that speeches which put their strongest arguments first are most persuasive.[13] There is questionable wisdom in a design that withholds the positive proposal to be advocated until after negatives have been dealt with. Communication research indicates that "when contradictory information is presented by a single communicator, material presented first tends to be more effective than are communications presented subsequently."[14] Research also indicates that "when an authoritative communicator plans to mention non-salient arguments contrary to the position he is advocating, it is more effective persuasion if he gives his own arguments first rather than second."[15] If these findings are true, useful design seems to call for the presentation of the advocated idea first, delaying any contrary data for subsequent examination in the light of the strong positive impression this first presentation has made.

Two other research conclusions cast doubt upon the universal advisability of climactic design. One states that "presentation of information that has to do with need satisfaction after need arousal occurs is superior to the reverse order." The other finds that "placing first the communication whose contents are highly desirable to the people involved is more effective persuasion than is the reverse order."[16] The first of these conclusions argues against the procedure of presenting an idea and only in the later part of the sermon building to a climax by painting a glowing picture of the needs it fulfills. Need arousal is an introductory rather than a concluding task. The second conclusion suggests the ineffectiveness of holding until last the idea most likely to seem desirable to the hearer. The more persuasive design appears to be that which begins with the more desirable and proceeds in a descending scale.

In the light of such data the principle may be restated: Points should be arranged in an ascending scale of affective impact;

but conceptual climax must be used with cautious regard for audience fatigue and the value of placing strong points first, placing the arguments of the speaker before opposing points, placing need arousal before need satisfaction, and placing more desirable before less desirable points.

Models That Implement Function

Design may well vary with the functional intent of the message. As the preacher reviews his completed worksheet, he may see an outline beginning to emerge. It might be suggested by the designated purpose. If the intent is to convince, for example, the outline may consist of a series of reasons why the main proposition commands belief. If it is to inform, an outline that explains the main idea, point by point, may be indicated. The worksheet review might suggest, however, that the *diagnosis* or *prescription* contains the seeds of an outline that proposes a strong idea and then shows, in successive major sections, how this idea comes to the aid of persons in different kinds of need. Or the outline might emerge from the exposition, as the text gives rise to several affirmations that claim attention as the salient points.

Sermon designs have become conventionalized into identifiable types of outlines, several of which the preacher might well fix in mind, not as prescribing molds into which his sermons must be poured but as alternative models to spark his own inventiveness and help him shape design to function.

1. *The two-point design* is one of the simplest. One of its uses is the case in which audience analysis reveals little or no awareness of the problem to which a solution is being offered, so that the speaker is under the necessity of apportioning at least half of his time to identifying and defining the problem. In this case the design may take the following form: (*a*) This is a problem we need to solve. (*b*) This is a promising solution. In David H. C. Read's sermon already considered, we saw another application of this design: (*a*) "Do we need a new religion?" (*b*) "Have you really tried the one you were given?" F. W.

Robertson's sermons almost habitually expressed this design in some form. His sermon on "The Power of Sorrow," from II Cor. 7:9, 10, dealt with (*a*) "The fatal power of the sorrow of the world," and (*b*) "The life-giving power of the sorrow that is after God." [17] Thus within the general type of the two-point design there is room for fluid variety combined with straightforward simplicity.

2. *The question design* may suggest its points in an interesting and undogmatic form. One lectionary selects Deut. 1:5, 8–18, as the Old Testament lesson for Independence Day. Studying it, the preacher finds helpful reflections on patriotism, together with indications of how the Biblical tradition grew, guiding Israel's life in a later period by a reappropriation of earlier insights, as if Moses were speaking to the new time. Naming his sermon "Weighed by Ultimate Concern," he designs it around three questions: (*a*) Are we keeping our conscience alert in Biblical perspective? (*b*) Are we seeking the truth by listening to those who most differ from us? (*c*) Are we fulfilling the trust committed to us as a people? Such an outline invites thoughtful response and may deal with difficult matters by a probing inquiry rather than a bald assertion.

3. *The ladder or telescope design* affords opportunity for a closely linked argument. The design may begin, like a ladder, on the lowest rung and climb, step by step, through a series of reasons to a conclusion. Or it may unfold, telescope-fashion, in a series of points, each of which picks up the closing term of the point before it and adds some further statement. In a Palm Sunday sermon from Luke 19:29–40, the preacher fixes attention on verse 40, "I tell you, if these were silent, the very stones would cry out," developing the idea that Christ challenges us by confrontation with reality too deep to be silenced. Dealing with the whole situation reflected in the Scripture, he develops a telescope design: (*a*) Christ comes to demand choice. (*b*) The choice centers in the cross as the final key to power. (*c*) The power of the cross defeats the enemies of our fullest life.

4. *The classification design* takes some embracing theme and shows its relevance to several different classes of situation, per-

son, or need. With the Easter gospel, Mark 16:1–7, before him, the preacher notices the force of the words, "He is going before you to Galilee; there you will see him." Galilee, he recalls, was the obscure outland of everyday work and commonplace trial for the disciples. It is there that the risen Christ meets us. Formulating his proposition to say that, in our everyday Galilee, Christ engages to keep his rendezvous in answer to our most urgent needs, he designs a classification sermon which declares that Christ will be present (*a*) in answer to death, (*b*) in answer to defeat, and (*c*) in answer to despair.

5. *The series-of-statements design* offers a sequence of sub-propositions that enlarge or support the main proposition. We have seen one vivid example in J. Wallace Hamilton's "What Is Communism Doing for Us?" It might be a useful design for a sermon on the transfiguration scene reported in Matt. 17:1–9. The preacher decides that the issue at stake in this passage is that of the nature of Christ's authority. In the introduction he makes a needed distinction between the authoritarian (which Christ refused to be) and the authoritative (which is based on intrinsic reality and awakened insight). His sermon then develops the theme "Christ's Final Authority" through a series of statements: (*a*) Christ has the authority of one who shows us who God is. (*b*) Christ has the authority of one who shows us who we were made to be. (*c*) Christ has the authority of one who points the way to our best future.

6. *The faceting or jewel design* cuts into a truth from various angles, as a jeweler cuts a gem, to reveal its worth as the light strikes it first one way and then another. Confronted by the reconciliation scene between Joseph and his brothers (Gen. 45:4–11) the preacher realizes that God's hand in the whole Joseph saga, with its tragedy and triumph, is suggested in the words, "Do not be distressed, or angry with yourselves, because you sold me here; for God sent me before you to preserve life." The issue in this story is the issue each of us must face: Does God really play a part in our affairs? It becomes, ultimately, the issue of whether our life has meaning and final hope. To rule out God's participation is to eliminate ultimate meaning; to lay

responsibility upon him is to prolong our immaturity. After long thought on the story and its message, the preacher formulates the proposition that *we* make history, but only in the presence of a God of sovereign grace. Cutting into that truth from several angles suggested by the text, he arrives at the design: (*a*) God works through providences appropriated by faith. (*b*) God works through a people obedient to his call. (*c*) God works through a presence encountered in life's depths.

7. *The Hegelian design* follows the dialectic progression through thesis, antithesis, and synthesis. It shows a truth from one side, then from its opposite, and finally from an angle that gathers strengths from both. Dealing with the Gospel for Passion Sunday according to his lectionary, the minister struggles with John 11:47–53, hinging on Caiaphas' words, "You know nothing at all; you do not understand that it is expedient for you that one man should die for the people, and that the whole nation should not perish." Recognizing that, in the Johannine method of thought, Caiaphas is used to reflect various strata of meaning, from the superficial to the profound, the minister gives special attention to the key word, "expedient"—politic, advisable, advantageous, practical. The Gospel seems to him to be saying that expediency, or practicality, presents varied faces among which we must choose. A modified Hegelian design seems best to develop the meaning: (*a*) Caiaphas followed a practicality that betrayed. (*b*) Jesus shows a practicality that saves. (*c*) We are called to a practicality that extends his ministry.

Conventionalized patterns should not be imposed on sermons; their usefulness is, rather, in suggesting alternative possibilities as the preacher ponders how he can best help listeners to get hold of the truth in ways that will make contact with the meanings already present in their minds. He must make a new design, fresh for every sermon. This creative undertaking can be a source of challenge and satisfaction, awaking the joy of craftsmanship and the exhilaration of struggle and achievement. In the process, his own awareness of the truth in the Gospel is quickened. To design sermons well, he needs to empathize, ever anew, with his listeners, putting himself in their place and trying to outline a message that meets their needs. When he has created a design that serves both them and the truth to be spoken, he is ready to encode it in ways calculated to whet their interest and creep inside their minds and motives. To that vital undertaking we shall turn in the next two chapters.

PROBES

1. Ilion T. Jones, *The Principles and Practice of Preaching* (Abingdon Press, 1956), Ch. 6, can reinforce your understanding of the types of outlines, by offering a different set of illustrative examples. W. E. Sangster, *The Craft of Sermon Construction* (The Westminster Press, 1951), Ch. 3, and Halford E. Luccock, *In the Minister's Workshop* (Abingdon Press, 1954), Ch. 13, give somewhat divergent models that you may find helpful. H. Grady Davis, *Design for Preaching* (Muhlenberg Press, 1958), Chs. 7–10, approaches the matter from a wholly different angle, also worthy of study.

2. There is value in familiarizing yourself with the way some strong preacher habitually attacks the problem of design (as in the case of F. W. Robertson, whose characteristic use of the two-point design we have noted). Select a preacher of established excellence—Fosdick, Hamilton, Read, Stewart, Armstrong, or some other whom you admire—and outline a half dozen of his sermons. What designs do you find him using? Does he have any characteristic type of outline to which he frequently returns? How much do his models vary? Does he evolve patterns that do not fall within the types we have classified? If so, how would you characterize them?

3. Outline a sermon developing one of the ideas worked out in the Probes for Chapter 11. First run through the types of design we have studied, to see if one of them is adapted to the needs of your material, and then use that type as a model on which to build your own creative thought pattern.

CHAPTER 13

Achieving
Interactive Interest

"The sin of being uninteresting is in a preacher an exceedingly mortal sin." [1] The large, bushy-haired man who had just written that sentence was putting a nationwide reputation—as widely read author, former college president, honored bishop—behind it. Was it true? he pondered. It was. He believed it so strongly that he took from it the title for a chapter on "The Sin of Being Uninteresting" in his major book of practical theology.

The year was 1910. So many acts then labeled sins have been revalued since, that the bishop's case for his contention should be reviewed. He argued that the gospel is so important and so packed with interest that to deal dully with it must be sin: The preacher ranges the Bible's landscape, the most varied on earth. He deals with the issues that recur throughout the drama of world history. He takes up the contests that have moved the most memorable orators. His is the exciting business of changing lives, proclaiming love, representing Christ. The sermon deals with the greatest story in the world and must be told fascinatingly. To do less is sin, the honored intellectual author and bishop maintained.

Sin or not, it is self-defeating. Interest precedes influence. If we make communication that matters, the listener must cooperate. The choice is his; he must *want* to hear what is being said. Achieving interactive interest is communication's *sine qua non*. We must ask now, What are its key skills and strategies?

Strategies That Arrest Interest

Some psychological guides can help us. Attention, at best, roves swiftly over a kaleidoscopic range. Whatever the individual's unique preoccupations, a contest for interested attention is waged in every mind. Six strategic factors can help in winning the prize.

1. *Intensity.* We notice a bright light rather than surrounding dimmer ones, a strong color among dull hues, a loud noise rather than the ticking of our watch, limburger cheese before cheddar.[2] In sermon delivery, intensity matters. Vocal variety in rate, pitch, and volume makes the preacher seem more alive and interesting. Vigorous body tone and gesture, with emphasis through eye contact, compel attention. These intensity factors lend a sense of personal weight to a delivery.

Intensity can characterize content as well as delivery. Concrete materials are more intense than abstractions. We may generalize about ecology, for instance—or we may speak of the day the polluted Cuyahoga River caught fire, or quote George Sanders' suicide note: "Dear World: . . . I am leaving you with your worries in this sweet cesspool—good luck." *Sweet cesspool* indeed! The intensity of that compels attention.

2. *Contrast and novelty.* The epigrammatic statement rivets attention. Jesse Jackson highlighted a problem easily lost from view when he capsulized "the psycho-linguistics of racism." "When we're unemployed," he quipped, "we're called lazy; when the whites are unemployed it's called a depression."[3] Similarly, terse examples and succinct stories can give the sharpness of novelty and contrast.

Statistical or historical data, adequately dramatized, can achieve this end. In the darkest days of World War II, Harry Emerson Fosdick reminded a dispirited congregation: "The year 1809 . . . was one of the most discouraging in Europe's history. Napoleon was dominant, as Hitler is now. His battles and victories were the absorbing news, and, evil as our times are, I suspect that to those who lived then, 1809 seemed as bad or worse. But think of what was going on in 1809 that was not in the news at all. In that year Charles Darwin was born. In that year Lincoln was born. In that year Gladstone was born, and Tennyson, and Edgar Allan Poe, and Oliver Wendell Holmes, and Cyrus McCormick, the inventor of the harvester, and Mendelssohn. At the very least, one must say that the world was not as hopeless as it looked." [4] Dramatized facts made hope persuasive in *contrast* with prevailing despair.

3. *Movement and change.* Attention is kinetic. What moves deflects the attention of even the most concentrated. The older orators knew the calculated value of walking across the platform when a baby cried or attention wandered; but movement can be more than physical. Thought must move. To keep it advancing is vital to interest. A well-aimed story can sometimes give the play of movement over aspects of a subject.

Helmut Thielicke, for example, swiftly ticked off salient points of his theme by narrating a conversation with a taxi driver. The driver's opening gambit, "I really believe in paganism," set the key. Thielicke asked, "Where, then, do you have your mascot doll hanging?" and the man pointed to his moneybag in the glove compartment, expressing surprise at having his habit of mind read so well. "Oh," said his passenger, "I can tell you a lot more than that. You don't like to drive on Fridays and furthermore, you're quite miserable if you have to start out on the thirteenth. You are also interested in astrology, and I would be willing to bet that more than once you've had your horoscope cast."

When the man, startled, asked, "How do you know all that?" Thielicke replied: "It's because I know my neopagans well. These people are very uneasy in a world without God; that's why they need all this stuff." [5] From this peripheral sparring, the conversation moved to some central issues of faith. Occupying about one fourth of the time of a fairly long sermon, it was neither ornament nor dramatic filler. Its swift *movement* kept the mind advancing toward the heart of the message.

4. *Repetition.* The varied twittering of robins outside your window may go unnoticed, but the insistently repeated call of a blue jay compels your attention. One researcher concluded from his experiments that two or three repetitions of a key statement near the beginning and/or the end of a speech fix attention more than do repetitions evenly distributed throughout the presentation.[6]

James S. Stewart made telling use of this device in a sermon on the Trinity, preached from II Cor. 13:14, which contended that "this doctrine impinges upon, and strikes home to, the experience of ordinary people like ourselves." "It began," he said, "when men made this discovery—that they could not say all they meant by the word 'God' until they had said Father, Son, Spirit." Within a matter of moments, in the fairly long introduction, he repeated that twice over: "You cannot say all that the mysterious word 'God' means for you, you cannot convey or describe what that transcendent name connotes, until you have said, Father, Son, Spirit." And again, "Is it not true that you cannot say all that is contained for you in the word 'God' until you have said Father, Son, Spirit?" [7] Thus concentrated *repetition* did much to make the message rememberable.

5. *Human interest.* People interest people. Persons, not stock figures, need to march through our material. Speech comes alive as it is personalized. Rudolf Flesch suggests a formula for estimating personal interest: "Count all personal names in your text. Then count all personal pronouns (except the *it's* and *they's* that don't refer to people). Next, count all masculine and feminine words such as "uncle" or "spinster" (but not masculine and feminine words such as "teacher" or "employee"). Finally, for good measure, count the two words "people" and "folks." Altogether, the percentage of these words (their number per hundred words of text) will give you a fairly good human-interest yardstick. . . . In good, readable nonfiction . . . it's usually around six or eight." [8]

Carl Stokes, for instance, interests us in his mayoral candidacy when he brings a conversation with his eleven-year-old son into his account of the decision to run again. "Last year I really had to think seriously about whether or not to run for reelection. The first year and a half was a tough period. I never dreamed it would be like that. So I sat down at the table with Carl, Jr., one morning. And I asked him, 'Carl, do you think I ought to run again?' And he said, 'Yes, I think you should.' And I said, 'Why?' He said, 'Well, I think you've done a pretty good job.' " [9] Stokes could have told us flatly that his family approved his candidacy and that he was running on his record. The words would have been fewer and the meaning the same, but the flat statement would not have riveted our attention as did this reported conversation with its strong, simple element of human interest.

6. *Internal values and wants.* Some wants are sufficiently universal to be predictable. The pastoral psychologist Edgar N. Jackson estimates that in any 100 people we might gather, 20 will be struggling with bereavement and grief, 33 with problems of marital adjustment, 50 with serious emotional turmoil, 20 with at least mild neuroses, and from 3 to 8 with guilt and loneliness based on homosexual impulses.[10] Messages that touch such widespread needs irresistibly trigger spontaneous interest.

Beyond these universals, each of us brings his own private world of interests to any listening encounter. The sensitive minister who uses the opportunities for audience analysis peculiar to his pastoral office, as noted in Chapter 4, can beam his message to these live, current concerns. As he touches their internal values and wants, many persons will find him "bowling down their alley"—not speaking vaguely "to whom it may concern."

Intensity, contrast and novelty, movement and change, repetition, human interest, and internal values and wants—appealing to these, we can awaken the hearer's interest and increase our chance of enlisting him as an active communication partner.

The Introduction Must Focus Interest

Interactive interest is won or lost in the introduction. Parenthetically, we do well to note, it must be rewon continuously,

from the first moments of a sermon to the last. One researcher, for instance, after holding a stopwatch on students as
they studied in a library, reported that about 40 percent of
their time was spent in "drawing doodles, watching others, gaz-
ing blankly into space." Some authorities reckon on a serious
lapse of attention in any auditor about every seven minutes.[11]
With attention so transient, it is obvious that interest must be
rewon continuously. Nevertheless, the opening words of a sermon afford a unique strategic opportunity.

The introduction must dispel the "Ho-hum, here we go again"
frame of mind. To do so, it must get quickly to material that
matters. No listener will long remain a cooperative communication partner if he is left without help in puzzling out answers to
his essential questions: *What* is the preacher talking about? and
Why does he bring that up? Over the shortest available route
the introduction needs (*a*) to give forceful statement to the
working subject, (*b*) to help the listener feel how and why the
subject is important to him, (*c*) generally to offer some statement of the proposition, and (*d*) to throw out some clue as to
the way the subject will be attacked. No catchy devices for
snaring the listener's interest will long avail if these basic communication needs are bypassed.

To get the hearer's attention is not enough; we must fix his
thought on the central matter of the hour. Attention-getting introductions on any other basis can frustrate the listener and
defeat the preacher. One sometimes hears a sermon that begins
with fascinating material aimed to evoke interest, and only after
some minutes of increasingly perplexed listening, discovers that
the idea suggested by the attention-arresting story is not the
idea the preacher is really discussing. Backtracking from where
the story seemed to point to where the preacher is heading, one
falls further behind the thought on the way. Attention captured
for its own sake means nothing; attention focused on the main
idea is essential.

For this reason, a framework sometimes prescribed for the
persuasive speech holds value. Instead of the traditional divisions
—introduction, body, conclusion—the literature of persuasion

sometimes calls for: introduction, *statement,* body, and conclusion. To reach a decision on any serious issue, an audience needs to have the proposal stated with some clarity before other steps in the persuasive process can progress far. The sermon, likewise, profits by a clear step of statement of its main idea, either as a part of the introduction or in some very early movement in its design.

Alternative Opening Gambits

Live, moving openings may be achieved by varied strategies. The preacher may begin with a *situation,* as does a dramatist when he opens a play not with a philosophical soliloquy, but with a swift cut into a slice of life in which some action is already under way. George A. Buttrick has frequently plunged into situations with his opening words. One Buttrick sermon begins, for example: "Rupert Brooke, taking ship from Liverpool to New York, felt suddenly lonely, for he seemed the only passenger without friends on the dock to wave him good-by. So he ran back down the gangplank, picked out an urchin, and asked, 'What's your name?' 'Bill,' said the boy. 'Well, Bill, you are my friend, and here is sixpence. Wave to me when the ship goes.' The boy waved a handkerchief in a very grubby hand. Our human voyage is a still lonelier affair." [12] That got swiftly to the heart of the matter through the gateway of a dramatic situation.

The introduction may open with *something that makes a crucial difference.* One of Wallace E. Fisher's sermons begins: "In a nation which likes to think of itself as the land of the free, it is jarring to learn that the President of the United States had to apologize to a foreign diplomat because a restaurant in Dover, Delaware, refused to serve him. Mr. K. A. Gbedemah, Finance Minister of the Negro republic of Ghana, was refused service because his skin is black." A recital of other crucial incidents led to a localizing of the issue: "We are not yet an integrated congregation. We have not matured to the point

where our members look on all people as *our* friends in Christ.
. . . This sermon aims to challenge and to encourage Trinity
Church in its rising concern for persons as *persons*." [13] From
the outset, it was clear that this sermon dealt with something
that *made a crucial difference* to those who heard it.

An introduction may begin with *an effect needing a cause*.
Nothing more arrests attention than a situation whose origin
mystifies us. If an important matter is thus unexplained, the
attention is the more captivated. This was the strategy of a
Fosdick sermon that began by pointing to a question raised by
Job's friends: " 'See!' they cry, 'thou art destroying religion.'
More than 2,000 years ago men were saying that." Two millen-
nia of that cry, and still religion persists. "What keeps religion
going?" "Who of us," Fosdick asked, "has not had some cher-
ished theological idea smashed to pieces, seen some old religious world view disintegrate, until we too cried, Thou art
destroying religion? Everyone here has used these words of the
friends of Job. Today we consider the fact that men have said
that from the beginning, and still religion goes on. What keeps
it going?" [14] As the unfolding sermon made persuasively clear,
the answer to that problem of an effect needing a cause gets at
some matters of foundational importance concerning the power
and truth of the gospel.

Occasionally an introduction can begin with *something startling*. Shock value can be overworked, but used judiciously it
crowds out other matters that compete for attention. James
Baldwin even stopped the inexorable clock of a television interview with a startling sentence. David Frost, as moderator, was
closing off the show with words that usually end all debate:
"That, alas, is all we've got time for," when Baldwin broke in
with: "I want to say one last thing. I would like to alert the
American people to this fact, that they're not after me, but after
you."

That was too much for Frost, who asked for an explanation.
"I think," said Baldwin, "for the first time the people legally
white and the people legally black are beginning to understand

that if they do not come together they're going to end up in the same gas oven." [15] Amazingly, though the time was gone, the interview went on to probe the meaning of that. James Armstrong employed a milder form of the technique of something startling when he opened a sermon by saying: "I am a radical; at least I try to be. To begin like that requires an explanation." [16]

Some introductions can begin with *a conflict*—which is the essence of drama. One playwright suggested that he makes plays by putting a character under pressure until he breaks open to show what makes him tick. The other part of that creative strategy lies in the fact that the pressure that breaks the character open is a play of forces against each other. The Bible's treasure-house of drama features all kinds of conflict: in its opening, God and the serpent; in the moments of tragic grandeur, God and the devil; in the contest on Calvary, love and hate, estrangement and reconciliation; in its closing thunders, God and the cosmic powers. Its peace is so snatched from conflict that it "passes all understanding." Its faith, far from a placid Sabbath mood, is "the victory that overcomes the world." Our life is beset by conflict and our faith thrives in conflict. Our sermons may well begin, from time to time, with the drama of that.

The Power of the Last Impression

Interactive interest must carry through the conclusion. The sermon needs to end persuasively, and one factor in making that possible is *direct suggestion*. The term has a background in hypnosis. The hypnotic subject is given some act to perform or attitude to express when he awakes. Carrying out this suggestion, he believes it to be his own idea and may give elaborate reasons for his behavior. Analogous to that, a suggestion planted in the conclusion of a sermon in which a strong case has been made and an empathic bond established between preacher and hearer may carry over beyond the immediate present. Studies comparing four factors—repetition, frequency, coexistence, and last impression—found that the last impression was the most important in creating powerful suggestion.[17] The persuasive conclusion employs this device, stating the sermon's main thrust with utter directness.

Most conclusions, in the mood of contemporary audiences, set a premium on brevity. There is a swift restatement of the main idea, some vivid material to clinch the point, and a strong closing sentence. Such was the nature of the conclusion of Arthur John Gossip's first sermon after the tragic death of his wife. Preaching on the question, "But When Life Tumbles In, What Then?" Gossip drew upon his own plunge into grief for resources to help his people in their times of sorrow. His conclusion is classic:

"I don't think you need to be afraid of life. Our hearts are very frail; and there are places where the road is very steep and very lonely. But we have a wonderful God. And as Paul puts it, what can separate us from His love? Not death, he says immediately, pushing that aside at once as the most obvious of all impossibilities.

"No, not death. For, standing in the roaring of the Jordan, cold to the heart with its dreadful chill, and very conscious of the terror of its rushing, I too, like Hopeful, can call back to you who one day in your turn will have to cross it, 'Be of good cheer, my brother, for I feel the bottom, and it is sound.'" [18]

A brief restatement of the theme, a strong direct suggestion, a piece of vividly colorful material to rivet attention once more, a vital closing sentence, and he was through. Such is the conclusion at its best—swift, strong, full of interactive interest to the last breath.

PROBES

1. For further reading, see Wayne C. Minnick, *The Art of Persuasion,* 2d ed. (Houghton Mifflin Company, 1968), Ch. 3, which treats "Attention—The Tuning Process" helpfully from the point of view of psychological and communication research;

and Ilion T. Jones, *The Principles and Practice of Preaching* (Abingdon Press, 1956), Ch. 9, which offers concise wisdom on "Preparing the Introduction and Conclusion."

2. Prepare an introduction for one of the sermon ideas you have in process, employing both the statement step advocated in this chapter, and one of the proposed "alternative opening gambits."

3. For the same sermon idea, prepare a conclusion, making use of direct suggestion and some brief, colorful material such as Arthur John Gossip used in his conclusion, quoted in this chapter, with its dramatic line from John Bunyan's *The Pilgrim's Progress*.

CHAPTER 14

Fashioning Substance That Communicates

Having formulated the dynamic idea and outlined the design of the message, how does the preacher mold materials that give it body, muscle, movement? Though popular discussion has often used the term "illustration" to designate such substance, more than illustration is involved. Illustration has its place: it puts pictures in the message; in a medium chiefly acoustic, it serves to make the ear another eye; it makes abstract matters concrete; it invites interest. Yet the concept "illustration" is too narrow for our purpose.

We might speak more adequately of "support material"—the whole web of fact, symbol, explanation, and evidence that gives substance to thought. In dealing with materials that relate the message to the meanings of the listener, this chapter will consider (*a*) material that clarifies meaning, and (*b*) material that supports belief. We will discuss how we find such material and make it available for use.

Meeting a Basic Need of the Mind

As a prior essential we must deal with the mind's need of a validly understood relation between the general and the particular. In this relation, which generates the dynamic idea, the sermon *begins*. We noted that the idea comes to life as an ellipse around two foci: the Biblical text and the contemporary human situation. Locating these foci plunges the preacher into the detailed study of particulars. He particularizes in his exegetical study of the text, grasping its meaning through his understanding of a body of data he digs out. He particularizes again as the study of contemporary axioms and the needs of his people sharpens his focus on the local human situation. Out of these particulars he formulates in a proposition sentence the generalized statement of the idea. Particularization inheres also in the design, which breaks the dynamic idea into its constituent parts.

Each major movement within a sermon continues this process. Preaching on "The Whereabouts of God," James Armstrong began with a generalized question and then particularized it. Armstrong asked, *"Where is God in such a world?"* He then broke that query down: "In us? In folk like us? In empty souls and shattered nerves and senses driven wild by film and ad and constant titillation?" That, however, does not give the question all the content it needs. Armstrong continued:

"Where is God in such a world? On streets of fear, where muggers lurk and rapists ply their trade? Where pickets march and scholars plead, and generations are separated by so much more than years?

"Where is God in such a world? In Birmingham, where police dogs strain against the leash, and snarl, and bare their teeth at trembling old ladies painted black by nature's brush?

"Where is God in such a world? In sniper's nest? In homemade bomb? In the mad shriek 'Burn, baby, burn,' as cities turn to ashes overnight?

"Where is God in such a world? In rocket and napalm? In earth that's scorched? In a village peasant's scream and a dying soldier's whimpering cry?

"Where is God in such a world? Where is God?" [1]

If the question had a generalized, remote ring when it was first asked, it bled and moaned with the stark particulars of human grief at its last asking. What followed in the developing sermon could not have been half so potent if the question had not become this web of insistent cries wrung out of particularized situations.

As a structure of serious thought the sermon is bound by the iron necessity of generalizations grounded in accurately observed particulars, and particulars that give substance and reality to its generalizations. Sermons that move only from one anecdotal particular to another seem trivial and leave the listener wondering what it was all about. Sermons that move abstractly from one generalization to another seem never to touch ground. They leave the listener with no data by which to test their truth. To fashion substance that communicates, we must keep the relationship between the general and the particular tight and true at every step of the way.

Particulars Clarify Meaning

Particulars can clarify the meaning of a generalized idea. Recall some cardinal truths about meanings as we have studied them. (*a*) Meanings are not in words. Words are sounds or signs that mean different things to different people; and meanings are in people. (*b*) People can learn new meanings. A change in thought or life is a new meaning learned. (*c*) To convey a known meaning or teach a new one, we must make contact with meanings people already have. (*d*) We do this with messages. We cannot transmit meanings, but messages only. The messages must make contact with the receiver's meanings to evoke new meanings and teach new responses. (*e*) Messages, therefore, must contain substance full of the particulars that can touch the meanings in the receiver's mind. As Emerson said to a preacher trying to help a troubled man by means of generalized abstractions, "Speak *things* to him, or hold your peace."

Particulars are essential to *denotative meaning*. Attempts to define leave us confused as we move from one abstract word to another. The word "homiletic," for instance, carries the dictionary definition: "of the nature of a homily; of or relating to homiletics." Not greatly helped, we look further for "homily,"

and find: "a religious discourse usually before a congregation."
Unless we already know a good deal about the subject, the word
is still swathed in vagueness. To give useful denotative meaning,
we need material that concretely "points" to a thing or an action
we can visualize.

In James Armstrong's quest for "The Whereabouts of God,"
for example, note the material that points. Armstrong tells us,
first, that God is in events, not forcing them to happen, but
inspiring some, judging all, and sharing their consequences
with us. "The God of Moses was the God of current events," he
says, and after a few swift words of explanation of that, he
breaks it down into particulars. With a sentence or two about
each, he tells us that "Moses' God is the God of covenant";
"He is the God of law"; "He is the God who works through
people." Then he says: "We mutter about preachers who dabble
in politics. We complain about religious cranks and zealots who
march and protest and become involved in controversy. Look
at Moses! That was no doddering old bishop he confronted.
That was the mightiest ruler of his time. And Moses cried: 'You
let my people go.' When his plea fell on deaf ears, he returned
to the victims of his nation's tyranny, identified with them, organized them, marched with them, and led them from their
bondage, pursued by troops that served under the flag of his
land. That wasn't a church council he was challenging, not a
vestry or a synod or an administrative board. That was the
Pentagon; that was the White House; that was the Establishment
of his day." [2]

Particulars tumble over each other. Illustration, in the sense
of little stories, or elaborate pictures, is not here. Yet the verbs
—"organized," "marched"—not only report something about
Moses, they evoke images of our own time. Phrases of like
evocative power—"no doddering old bishop," "victims of his
nation's tyranny," "pursued by troops," "that was the Pentagon"
—perform their "pointing" function. We see the denotative
meaning of Moses' God as "the God of current events."

No less essential are particulars in conveying *connotative meaning,* which relates an experience to us personally. This internalized meaning carries a heavy load in religious communication. Between the coldly factual and the maudlin sentimental, the effective middle ground is not easily occupied. For this purpose we need particulars that keep us close to direct experience.

Note how Armstrong accomplishes this in "The Whereabouts of God." Having generalized that "God became real in an event, the Christ-event," he proceeds from that to some "conclusions about God," the first of which is that "God is love." "What does that mean?" the preacher asks. "Well," he answers, "how does love respond to the hated Samaritan (or was he a Puerto Rican?); to the loose, immoral woman (or was she a homosexual?); to the screaming madman (a paranoid husband? a neurotic wife?). Love is not a concept to be debated; it is an acceptance of the rejected." [3]

Love is not sentimentalized, yet one feels its warmth. The paired particulars keep the text-situation ellipse constantly before us: "hated Samaritan (or was he a Puerto Rican?) . . . immoral woman (or was she a homosexual?) . . . screaming madman (a paranoid husband? a neurotic wife?)." Each of these phrases is evocative. Deeply felt by the preacher, each can be deeply felt by the listener. Definite, concrete, yet not drawn in much detail, they leave the listener free to fill in his own connotative meanings.

Every sermon needs particulars, drawn sufficiently to the life to point to denotative meanings with explanatory power, and touching inner experiences in ways that call forth the strongly felt connotative meanings of the listener and conscript them in the service of new meanings the gospel seeks to impart.

Particulars Support Belief

Beyond this service, *particulars serve to support belief.* The preacher is not primarily a debater. He heralds good news which, when understood and brought into living contact with personal experience, wins its way. Yet preaching also serves as apologetic. It answers attacks against the faith; it deals with men's doubts. In this task it employs sturdy particulars.

Think, for instance, of Harry Emerson Fosdick's sermon on "Christian Faith—Fantasy or Truth?" preached in answer to the accusation, widely bandied about at the time, that religion is shown false by its rootage in the psychological need for wish fulfillment. Fosdick's first answer to that canard was an appeal to facts. Asking, "Since when has great religion been primarily pleasant and comfortable anyway?" [4] he placed in evidence a series of particulars. Orthodoxy, he recalled, has often been so uncomfortable that Henry Ward Beecher challenged the doctrines of his day, "insisting, as he put it, that God is not a thunderstorm that has to be approached under an umbrella." [5] New Testament religion, he declared, is so far from being chiefly comfortable that any review of the ministry of Jesus must move over a stern road of suffering to the accompaniment of the call, "If any man would come after me, let him deny himself and take up his cross and follow me." Of Gandhi, then at the height of his career of religious as well as political influence, he drew a vivid thumbnail sketch that gave point to his observation, "God has not so much saved Gandhi from trouble; God has got Gandhi into trouble." [6] Quoting from one of Whittier's serene hymns, he contrasted it with the poet "going to speak at an anti-slavery meeting, facing a crowd on the way that pelted him with rotten eggs until his black Quaker coat ran yellow with the stains." [7] Concluding this first section of the four-point sermon, Fosdick gathered his evidence into the generalization: "When we find a man who has deeply entered into the Christian faith, we find a man who has discovered not fallacious comfort but a deep, demanding seriousness in life." [8] In each of the succeeding sections there was a parallel piling of particulars placed in evidence.

Fashioning substance to support belief calls for care. Evidence is valid only when it has *relevance* and *reliability*. We gain relevance by an accurate assessment of the problem. Even slightly to misread the situation to which we must speak is to invite evidence which, however impressive in itself, is brought to bear on matters it does not truly meet. Regardless of its relevance, evidence is of only such worth as its reliability gives it. Fosdick's case carried weight because of the qualified witnesses he called: Henry Ward Beecher in contest with an overly severe orthodoxy; Gandhi, spiritual giant, hailing God as "the most exacting personage in the world and the world to come";[9] Whittier, revered poet and honored abolitionist, finding in religion "not first of all a search for comfort, but a search for righteousness and truth";[10] and the Christ of Gethsemane and Golgotha. The case required evidence from witnesses (*a*) who were of unquestioned spiritual stature, and (*b*) who had paid a price for their convictions. If he were vulnerable on either of these counts, a witness would be worthless, whatever the dramatic appeal of material about him. Fosdick's witnesses met the tests of relevance and reliability.

We have seen that one way to deal with deeply entrenched prejudices is to introduce facts that set up tensions that need to be resolved. This strategy of *dissonance* can sometimes induce change where direct argument would be rejected or reinterpreted as support of the prejudiced position. From time to time the dissonant data can be dropped into the context of the prejudice, and the preacher can occasionally suggest a new position that would relieve the tension thus created. Without engaging in combat that would be almost surely lost, he can thus, over a period of time, have some possibility of effecting change. To do this, however, he must bring to bear upon the entrenched attitude material that is concrete, relevant enough to create the needed discomfort with the old position, and so vivid as to be hard to dismiss.

Factual data of many kinds may serve to support belief, but in the realm of spiritual struggle and conviction *personal testimony* is most persuasive. Religious commitment, ultimately, grows not so much from logical demonstration as from the discovery of a position that makes victorious sense of life's struggle.

Paul, for example, may not always carry us captive to his logic; but his personal testimony strikes us with telling impact. He speaks of brutal beatings, stonings, and shipwreck. "I have been constantly on the road; I have met dangers from rivers, dangers from robbers, dangers from my fellow-countrymen, dangers from foreigners, dangers in towns, dangers in the country, dangers at sea, dangers from false friends. I have toiled and drudged, I have often gone without sleep; hungry and thirsty, I have often gone fasting; and I have suffered from cold and exposure." (II Cor. 11:26–27, NEB.) When, against that background, we hear him say, "I have strength for anything through him who gives me power" (Phil. 4:13, NEB), his personal witness carries us where his abstract arguments could not.

Negative testimony also convicts. In one of Studs Terkel's interviews, a young woman, highly paid in a comfortable job, remarks: "I'm very bored. I really don't know how I feel. . . . I can't think of anyone I love or respect. I can't be bothered with the news. . . . I can't care less. . . . My interest in life is me." [11] In such negative testimony of self-protective boredom one hears convincing echoes of Jesus' words, "Whoever seeks to gain his life will lose it" (Luke 17:33).

Biographical literature—not hagiographic portraits of the pious—abounds in testimony. Wherever human life is vividly portrayed by those who have observed with keen eye and written with sensitive feeling, material awaits the preacher. Whether testimony affirms victory against the background of struggle or rings with denials wrung from bitterness—this matters little so long as it takes the preacher deeply into the labyrinths of the heart. Negative or positive, it aids accuracy in diagnosis of human need and, soon or late, speaks to a preaching issue. The sensitive reader of biographies, autobiographies, personal letters and journals, firsthand accounts of adventure and exploration, history, and the works of the better interviewers, has an unfailing source of material drenched in human struggle, frustration, and achievement, from which he can draw testimony that supports belief.

Along with factual evidence and personal testimony we should note material that re-creates vivid experiences. Drawing the listener into its texture and feeling, such material creates vicarious experience or helps people to relive similar experiences they may have known. It carries the persuasiveness of something felt on one's own pulse. Here again, Fosdick supplies a moving example, as he points to how war, poverty, "slums, and all our social cruelties . . . kill decisive babies."

Listeners share vivid experience as Fosdick continues: "In 1805 Napoleon bombarded Vienna. . . . The shells burst everywhere, and one of them struck the Jesuit Grammar School, falling in the stone-flagged corridor, and blasting walls and windows. One of the students, an eight-year-old boy, was in his room practicing on the piano, and in terror he fell to the floor and hid his face. Then in a moment came the voice of one of the schoolmasters, calling through the ruined corridor: 'Schubert, Franz Schubert, are you all right?' So nearly did war take its toll of a decisive child." [12] Twice, in two succeeding paragraphs, Fosdick drives home his point with that recurring refrain, "Schubert, Franz Schubert, are you all right?" until it becomes a haunting experience for the listener. In that lived particularization the tragic cliché that war destroys children regains persuasive power.

Time to Assimilate Particulars

Thus to relate the general and the particular requires good workshop procedures. The relationship thrives best when sermons issue from long growth. A well-stocked file can supply a quickly carpentered sermon with an abundance of glib material, but the organic wholeness of generalizations and particulars that flow into each other like the sap in the roots and branches of a great tree is lacking. For such wholeness the preacher needs methods that permit ideas to germinate and slowly mature, nurtured by repeated reflection and sustained by materials drawn from subconscious depths.

Preachers who tap such springs of power almost invariably work by some system of longtime planning. For some, the plan is laid out in a definite schedule, with theme and Scripture fixed for each Sunday for many months or for the coming year.

For others, the plan is less scheduled but no less articulate in the planting and steady cultivation of ideas. Preachers who work in this way invest loving labor in notebooks in which sermons are in various stages of preparation. An idea is entered in the notebook when it first lifts its head and has little treasure of associations gathered around it. From time to time, the preacher records from his reading and experience new items that speak to the emerging idea. Reviewing the notebook frequently, such a preacher jots down other reflections. From week to week, the idea that seems ripest and most current is picked and prepared for sharing with the congregation. Whether by such informal methods or by a full-blown yearly schedule, sermons that keep the particular-general relation tight and true come by long growth.

Each preacher must find a method that fits his mind, by which to capture material and keep it available. Some ministers use highly elaborated filing systems; others find these an encumbrance too unwieldy to be useful. Other things being equal, the system that is simplest leaves most energy, undiverted by mechanics, available for creative work. Many preachers mark their books as they read, writing their own personal index of items, suggestive for their uses, on the flyleaves. Some preachers of great stature have combined with this simple device a habit of dropping into a desk drawer assorted clippings and brief notes of ideas and sources. Frequent leafing through such a collection has combined with an attentive memory to make the material available on call.

For some preachers a simple system of filing, keyed to the year's preaching program, proves useful. The schedule of themes and Scriptures for the year is typed on a master list, with dates and serial numbers for all themes. Parallel with this list, a set of file folders is prepared, each bearing the theme and serial number on its label. As reading, reflection, and passing experiences yield items that seem to be worth recording, the preacher turns quickly to his master list and finds the theme with which the new entry might best fit. On card or scratch pad he jots down a few words to recall the idea and indicate the source, saving time by heading the card with the serial number instead of the theme. In a morning's study he lets these slips accumulate on his desk, taking a moment at lunchtime to drop each into its numbered file. Week by week, as he takes up the file for the new sermon, he finds a little trove of gathered treasure on which to begin his work. At the end of the year his file is exhausted and he must begin again, but in any year's file the material is fresh with the vitality of new discovery. What is lost in comprehensive coverage of all possible subjects is gained in timely vigor.

By whatever system, the preacher needs to be about the business of gathering material, recognizing two prime essentials. First, he must articulate some relation between a particular item and the general it supports. There is no such thing as a "sermon illustration"; there are only illustrations or support materials for specific ideas or truths. Making the relationship firm from the start promises the most telling use of good material. The second essential is some plan that assures time for sermons to assimilate their support. Given that, the preacher can read widely, free from "cramming" for next Sunday, draw on accrued funds of substance that communicates, and move confidently into the preparation of each new sermon, assured that ideas will not want for the support by which they come alive.

PROBES

1. In further examination of the particular-general relation, see H. Grady Davis, *Design for Preaching* (Muhlenberg Press, 1958), Ch. 4. *The Craft of Sermon Illustration* (The Westminster Press, 1950), by W. E. Sangster, is worthy of thought-

ful reading. For important guidance on the use of evidence, testimony, and re-created experience, see Wayne C. Minnick, *The Art of Persuasion*, 2d ed. (Houghton Mifflin Company, 1968), Chs. 5, 6, and 9.

2. In this chapter we have analyzed some ways in which James Armstrong and Harry Emerson Fosdick have related generalized statement to supporting particulars. It would be useful for you to make your own analytical study of some of the sermons of strong preachers, to see how they used this relationship in clarifying meaning and supporting belief. Sermons of J. Wallace Hamilton, George Buttrick, and Gerald Kennedy, as well as of Armstrong and Fosdick, would serve well for this purpose.

CHAPTER 15

Evolving a
Communicative Style

"You have got a style before you have got a story—
and God help you." So H. G. Wells is said to have responded
to a young writer's insistent appeal for evaluation of his work.
When either writer or preacher gets style before story, it is only
decorative pose. Authentic style roots in the man's own distinctive perception and point of view. Seeing with his own integrity,
he speaks with his own flavor.

Of a beloved preacher people sometimes say, "He cannot
preach a dull sermon." The remark refers to more than skill in
weaving a tapestry of words. Beyond sparkling expression, people value such a preacher's message—rooted in firsthand encounter with the gospel, alive to their current needs, crafted with
workmanlike care. For such a man, style is multilayered:
wrought by hard-earned skill in expression, personal relation
to the message and its materials, and inner wholeness and force
that shape the message as this man, and no other, ought to
deliver it.

Linguistic Canons of Style

The Earl of Chesterfield remarked that "style is the dress of
thoughts." [1] The matter runs deeper, yet it is important that
thoughts be well dressed. Traditional treatments of style have
dealt largely with language, [2] and we may properly take up the

subject at this level, considering the classic canons of purity, precision, clarity, energy, beauty, and naturalness.

Purity refers to law-abiding respect for the rules of grammar and good usage. It is no accident that an excellent modern manual of style (by Strunk and White) devotes two thirds of its pages to elementary rules of usage and composition. Because some writers who enjoy a brief vogue in religious circles make a career of cultivating eccentricities—coined words, usages according to their private and undefined meanings, a diet of non-sentences with subject or verb missing—it is easy for younger colleagues to fall into these habits. This, they assume, is the idiom of the time; one must speak thus to be heard. But such usage heightens ambiguity and makes the language a less accurate tool of thought. A carpenter's contempt for workers who carelessly blunt their tools gives the cue; language is the preacher's tool, and today's usage that makes the tool less efficient for tomorrow's work is destructive of the craft. Abraham Lincoln's pure style, developed on the frontier to speak to unschooled crowds, demonstrates that one need not depress the language to speak to the masses.

Precision is the term for scrupulous accuracy. Speech need not be technical to be true; short, common words can express profound thoughts. But imprecise speech cannot communicate exact meanings, and inexact speech reflects blurred thought. He who has paid the price of precise thought can find the way to accurate expression.

Clarity names the act of making our meaning plain. Not much is achieved by a sermon, whatever its truth or beauty, if its meaning is not clear. Someone at his wits' end listens for a word that may give him a new grip on his troubled life, but little is accomplished without clear meaning. In the first century, Quintilian declared, "Care should be taken, not that the reader *may* understand, but that he *must* understand"; and in the nineteenth century, Spurgeon could still say, "It is not enough to be so plain that you can be understood; you must so speak that you cannot be misunderstood." Such speech comes only by disciplined work.

Energy points to saying the thing with force. Briefer words have more drive than polysyllables. As Oliver Wendell Holmes put it: "I would never use a long word where a short one would answer the purpose. I know there are professors in this country who 'ligate' arteries. Other surgeons only tie them, and it stops the bleeding just as well." [3] Shorter sentences have more force. "In composing," wrote Sydney Smith, "as a general rule, run your pen through every other word you have written; you have no idea what vigor it will give your style." [4]

Beauty differs from decoration. The lean style is often most pleasing to the ear, as beautiful architecture is structure, not ornate facade. Yet with sinewy grace speech can combine well-turned rhythms and sonorous words.

Naturalness names the quality of fitness in speech exactly right for the moment. It fits the thought, seems to "belong" in the context of the speaker's life and mind, is neither out of reach nor too elementary for the hearer, and is appropriate to the occasion. It grows out of a cultivated mind, natural and at ease because it is ready and inwardly whole. It fits the occasion and the minds of others because empathy and tact have been long cultivated. It is appropriate to the thought because long preparation has made the speaker at home with ideas, able not only to grasp their content but to *feel* their texture.

Style Through Disciplined Rewriting

Much can be done to cultivate a communicative style. We can write and rewrite. As a pianist's mastery is achieved, not by tripping through a composition from beginning to end but by drill on phrases patiently repeated over and over, the practice that builds style costs writing, blue-penciling, and patient writing again.

Preaching is chiefly oral expression; why, then, such stress on writing? Because the more deliberate pace of the pen chastens the headlong tongue. Many preachers who have spoken forcefully to throngs, often with few notes or none, have testified that they thought best with a pen in hand. When a preacher has written every word of a sermon, he has some assurance that he has thought it through in full. His manuscript may be left behind when he delivers the message, but it has served him and his people well by giving shape and coherence to his thought. Constant, painful writing offers those who speak much in public the best insurance against mere garrulity.

A preacher's writing is for the ear. That fact imposes its own restraints. Those who read what is written can pause to ponder or return to reread. Those who only hear what is said must go at the speaker's pace or not at all. For them, complex sentences become labyrinths in which they are lost; key matters stated only once may be obscured by a distracting noise or a wandering thought; high-flown words may hide meaning. Writing for the ear, the preacher keeps his sentences brief and direct, his words simple, his main ideas in unmistakable evidence by statement and restatement, and his staple language not adjectives and adverbs but nouns and verbs. "The adjective hasn't been built that can pull a weak or inaccurate noun out of a tight place." [5]

Two expedients can go far toward making speech easily understood. We can break up long sentences, and we can substitute words with fewer syllables for those with many. Rudolf Flesch has worked out a formula for testing ease of reading in material by counting average sentence length and the number of syllables per hundred words.[6] For a simple demonstration let us test the first paragraph of the preface to a book now a generation old. It reads:

"As the introduction points out, this book is an attempt to make it clear that the decisive and definitive embodiment of God in human life, in the person of Jesus Christ, is the heart and the centre of radiation for the entire Christian faith, experience, life and theology. It has long been the fact that minimizings of this belief tend to destroy the richness and wholeness of Christian faith; and in recent years, the rather jejune 'liberalisms,' as they have been called, have shown that they were inadequate to the fullness of the life which the Christian community imparts, while the sheer discontinuities of the so-called 'neo-orthodoxy' have also, but for other reasons, been unsatisfactory." [7]

The issues this paragraph raises have receded into history; our concern is only with the clarity of its prose. In its 115 words there are only two sentences; three, if one counts as two the major clauses separated by a semicolon. This yields an average sentence length of more than 30 words. Combined with the count of 167 syllables in the first 100 words, it produces a reading-ease quotient of about 35 on Flesch's 100-point scale. Now let us rewrite the paragraph in shorter sentences and fewer syllables. It might read:

"Christians know God through Jesus Christ. Everything radiates from him: life, faith, theology. This book tries to make that clear. To play this truth down has been to make Christian faith less rich and whole. In recent years 'liberals' have not been able to nurture the mind or build the full life of the Christian community. Nor has so-called 'neo-orthodox' teaching, with breaks in its thought, been able to satisfy."

In this form, the paragraph contains seven sentences with an average of 11 words each. The syllable count has dropped from the original 167 to 102. On the 100-point scale the reading-ease quotient is now 96. Yet little that the original paragraph said has been lost. The change has come about by using only two devices: breaking up long sentences, and substituting words of fewer syllables for those with many.

The preacher who would make his style understandable may well give himself to practice in these two devices, both when he writes and when he rewrites what he first set down. The prose that seems simple and easy is often that which has been worked out by the longest toil. Tennessee Williams achieved the easy dialogue of his plays by taking them through as many as four or five drafts, and a page of final draft might have a dozen changes penned into its typescript. It was hard work, but Williams responded to an interviewer's question by saying: "The hours in the studio are the high point of my day. They're what my day is for, you know? The rest is just passing time as agreeably as possible. But the writing is the challenge and excitement of the day." [8] Making the gospel clear and winsome cannot be less vital.

The "Expressive" Style of the Involved

Beyond craftsmanship with words, style—as Georges de Buffon said—"is the man himself." The manufactured public relations image obscures this truth. One of the guiding memos of the 1968 presidential campaign said, in part: "It's not what's there that counts, it's what's projected, and we must be very clear on this point, that the response is to the image, not the man, and that this response often depends more on the medium and its use than it does on the candidate himself." [9] This may be true for a distant figure whose contacts with everyday people are carefully stage-managed; it is neither possible nor desirable for the parish minister, whose work is validated by his life at close range among the people. For him "the style *is* the man himself."

We see this in his relation to the message he delivers. James M. Wall applies to film criticism categories that suggest much with regard to style in preaching. He speaks of experiencing film on a continuum from the "discursive" to the "presentational." At the "discursive" end of the continuum, attention is absorbed by what the film is *about:* plot, character portrayal, message. "On the other hand, when a film reaches us primarily at the presentational end of the continuum, we are not so much concerned with the information it may impart or the plot it may develop. We focus instead on the vision that the film projects. Because the film lends itself readily to this kind of perception, it has a greater potential for involvement with the viewer. It is more personal. It functions at the level of engagement." [10]

Antonioni's style, for instance, is not so much the straightforward telling of a story as the sharing of an experience in which actual events and fantasies merge—as, indeed, they do in real life for most of us. In such films we are drawn to the "presentational" end of the scale. We are involved not merely with plot but with the picture itself. We leave the theater with more than the recollection of being entertained; our minds are set to work and new evaluations of experience are asked of us.

Charles L. Rice applies a similar continuum to sermon evaluation.[11] At the "discursive-projective" extreme, "the preacher . . . projects a personality while remaining impersonal. . . . The discursive style evades human experience and superficial emotionalism parodies the human situation. . . . Human life is seen as raw material rather than as the very locus of the Incarnation." [12] Over against these " 'gotten-up' pieces," Rice places "expressive" preaching, based on the assumption "that truth must have a biographical, not a merely ideological context." [13] It is "expressive" because it draws directly on the life and experience of the preacher, confesses his own fears and needs, not merely his assurance and victory, and thus goes beyond objective dealing with material to a personal engagement with persons. Like the "presentational" experience of film, it involves the listener. This occurs because the preacher is himself involved.

We see the expressive style in a seminarian's sermon. It opened with an account of the preacher's recent late evening ride on a commuter train. His seatmate was an old man who asked, "Mister, you got the time?" "Was '12:05' the right answer?" the preacher wondered. "I had a book I wanted to read. I wanted to look over some notes I'd taken during the past week. I wanted to think, maybe to sleep a little." He confessed his withdrawal from the old man's obvious need to talk, putting his aloofness under judgment by interweaving incidents from the Gospels in which Jesus, with much to do, found time for unpromising people.

"So much to do," he said, "so much to see, so many hungers to satisfy, I want to feel it and hug it and smell it and taste it all, all of it . . . but . . . 'Mister, you got the time?' I want to make enough, and know enough, and laugh enough, and

climb up high enough to leave my mark for all to see . . . but
. . . 'Mister, you got the time?' So we must choose what we've
got time for simply because we have not got time for everything."

After some incisive Biblical and theological reflection on the
crucial nature of time as *kairos,* the preacher said: "I didn't
know it then, but I think I do now, that what that old man . . .
was saying really . . . was something about himself. . . . All
I did was nod and shrug, and we both died a little." The preacher
talked of how we need to listen "with more than our ears" and
see "with more than our eyes," and of how, later in the trip, the
old man had leaned over to ask wistfully, "How long will it take
from here?" "Jesus must have wondered about that too," he said.
" 'How long will it take from here?' Well, I am sure I don't
know. I only know it is a question I must struggle with and so,
if we take Jesus seriously, must we all." [14]

Going away from the service, the worshiper could identify
points the preacher had made, but these objective statements
were not the chief impact of the experience. Something personal
had happened. The preacher had opened himself to the congregation, and in response, one who was listening felt more
disposed to open his own heart and look within it. Questions
had been raised about time and our use of it and about our
sensitive relations to others. These questions came back haunt-
ingly in succeeding days. An involved preacher had involved
those who heard him. In such style a whole man, with his failures, but also with his convictions and his love, comes to expression.

"This is the eternal origin of art," wrote Martin Buber, "that
a human being confronts a form that wants to become a work
through him. Not a figment of his soul but something that
appears to the soul and demands the soul's creative power." [15]
In strong preaching the truth of the gospel and the depth of
human experience thus confront us and ask something of us.
Responding, the preacher does not so much *produce* something
as yield himself up, captivated. In the ensuing struggle to pre-

pare and deliver a sermon, he labors creatively; yet when he has finished, the sermon is not so much the telling of something he has known all along as it is the utterance of truth discovered in the process. He preaches well because some facet of the gospel has come freshly and powerfully to him, and his sermon rings with the glad surprise of what has been thrillingly made new. There is toilsome craftsmanship in the preparation, but there is also a glimpse of what is most essentially real in the man's experience. Such preaching is involving, because it wells up from the deepest core of the being of a man who is himself involved.

PROBES

1. An important handbook is William Strunk, Jr., *The Elements of Style,* revised by E. B. White (The Macmillan Company, 2d ed., 1972). A larger guide to keep within arm's reach is Wilson Follett, *Modern American Usage,* edited and completed by Jacques Barzun *et al.* (Hill and Wang, 1966). Two manuals by Rudolf Flesch, used as guides for diligent practice, can increase the clarity, warmth, and force of a minister's expression. They are *The Art of Plain Talk* (Harper & Brothers, 1946) and *The Art of Readable Writing* (Harper & Brothers, 1949).

2. Select a paragraph of difficult prose from one of your textbooks, and practice rewriting it in shorter sentences and words of fewer syllables. You can effect useful changes by recasting phrases to avoid the use of affixes—as when the sample in this chapter changed "richness" to "rich," "wholeness" to "whole," "liberalisms" to "liberals," etc. You can also simplify by using synonyms: "play down" for "minimizings," etc.

3. Go through a sermon or paper you have written, applying the same rewriting technique. This can be a useful exercise and an invaluable habit. (Too cumbersome? Ernest Fremont Tittle customarily wrote each of his masterful sermons in full, four times, and then preached without the manuscript!)

CHAPTER 16

Getting the
Message Heard

"The essential elements in the preaching situation on the human side," wrote John Knox, "are the preacher and the congregation; the sermon is not a third element, but the action of one of the elements on the other, or, better perhaps, the movement of one of the elements toward the other. If the sermon as a distinct element comes into view, so that the preacher is thinking not about the congregation and what he wants to say to them, but about the sermon he prepared last week, the words of which lie before him in a manuscript or have been memorized, and if the congregation has the impression that it is hearing, not the preacher but this same sermon—in such a situation authentic preaching is not taking place. A sermon is not a literary essay; it is an act of oral communication. And yet it must be carefully prepared, planned not alone in its general outline but as regards its very language. Must it not be agreed then that the central problem in the technique of preaching is how to make such preparation without impairing the direct and personal character of preaching itself?" [1]

That is the dilemma in getting the message heard. A gospel with its own claim, as truth, transcending preacher and hearer, comes to us with its liberating news and its call for response. Yet it has come through the personal perception of the preacher, and any change it evokes must issue from the meeting of the meanings of preacher and hearer. How to be faithful to this claim within the dynamics of the personal encounter is the question with which we must deal in the delivery of the sermon.

Meeting Communication Needs

Since the matrix of the Word in preaching is personal encounter, our initial guidance must come from an understanding of personal hungers the listener brings to the meeting. We are neither disembodied intellects, poised to consume ethereal logic, nor are we bundles of sentiment to be moved by trumped-up emotional ploys. Despite all intellectual self-sufficiency we need personal renewal through hearing the gospel declared as personal reality by another person; and the declaration must ring true to the whole range of personal experience—intellectual, emotional, practical.

William L. Malcomson has described twelve "communication needs" he finds personally important.[2] Though he makes no claim for their universality (he invites his reader, indeed, to make his own personal list), they merit careful consideration. The list of needs and responses given in Table II has been reworked and greatly abbreviated from Malcomson and therefore can convey only part of the flavor of Malcomson's treatment.

Wide is the range of needs that must be taken into account in creating the personal relationship between preacher and listener through which meanings can helpfully meet. "To take our place with others," writes a distinguished social psychologist, "we must perceive each other's existence, and reach a measure of comprehension of one another's needs, emotions and thoughts."[3] Useful consideration of sermon delivery is grounded far more truly in such awareness of the human situation than in the mechanics of voice formation, gesture, and the like.

Amid his reflections on expression through language, Joost Meerloo remarks that "a perfectly correct declaration of love is poor courtship. Music, flirtation and good food make us more eloquent."[4] A perfectly correct statement of the gospel, by the

Table II. COMMUNICATION NEEDS AND RESPONSES

What the Listener Needs	How the Preacher Can Respond
Recognition: one who knows and values my presence.	Shows respect by caring that I am there; gives something of worth, carefully prepared.
Presence: a group gathered in shared concern around a common cause.	Creates a sense of potential as a congregation, not a mere audience.
Listening: another person who is attentive to me.	Shows sensitive awareness of the opinions and feelings of others.
Dialogue: interactive openness in which to give and receive contributions.	Reveals his own urgency and his expectation of response, inward or overt.
Contribution: to know another needs me as a person, not as an organizational digit.	Points out concrete needs to be met and responses within my capacity to make.
Therapy: help in knowing who I am, given by one whose right to do so I recognize.	Comes as a whole person with "personal counseling on a group scale"; is open for individual counsel.
Judgment: to be told by one I respect, and who takes me seriously, where he thinks I have missed the way.	Speaks frankly about matters on which he has earned the right to a concerned opinion.
Hope: possibilities beyond the dark present, pointed by those who have found the way through.	Shares—from his own experience or others' experience, authentically reported—fruits of living deeply.
Commitment: a common goal shared with one who accepts me and seeks acceptance from me.	Reflects such commitment and evokes it from the group.
Information: significant facts and events I probably would not get from books.	Interprets events and persons—Biblical, historical, and current—with concern for them and for me.
Entertainment: the human lift of seeing another make full use of his abilities.	Enhances my sense of my own humanity by his serious craftsmanship of mind, voice, and manner.
Solitude: others who respect my need (and theirs) to be left free to make decisions.	Amid all his earnest concern, respects my need to work out my own ultimate solution.

same token, may be poor preaching. Personal warmth and integrity are required, together with concerned contact of eye with eye, openness to the listener that tells of the preacher's concern for him and whatever interests or injures him, and a multitude of nonverbal cues through body, face, and voice timbre. Painstaking verbal preparation of the sermon is vital, but its capacity finally to communicate is advanced or impeded by the preacher's sensitivity or disregard for these subtle factors of personal relationship.

Delivering a Whole Person

The relationship between persons becomes persuasive as a whole person presents the message. We have noted the crucial multichannel nature of most communication. As we deal with the delivery of the sermon, or any "preaching event," we need to ask what the preacher said with his face, what he said with his body, what he said with his words, and whether the visual, vocal, and verbal messages agreed.

Gestures are more than movements of the hands. Watching a vigorous speaker at work, you see the nod and tilt of the head imparting emphasis, mobility of facial expression reflecting changes in the feeling tone, the inclining of the torso to support hand gestures, and changes of stance that mark transitions in thought and emotion. Expressive gesture may be the subtle raising of an eyebrow, or it may involve the whole body, as when a quick half step back and the lifting of the hands accompany surprise or disagreement.

Inhibition of the spontaneous expression of feeling tends to increase with higher education. The college- and seminary-trained minister, as a consequence, needs to free himself for the full nonverbal accompaniment of his message. It is as important to clear one's facial expressions of ambiguities and contradictions as to clarify one's sentences. Studying their own images, as recorded on videotape, has helped many preachers; for those who lack such facilities, speaking before a mirror can afford opportunity to learn something of the impression created by various gestures. Remembering that athletes and artists of the dance improve through such self-analysis and that the nonverbal channels carry an important message load, the preacher need not let notions of artificiality restrain him from similar self-study.

There is a word of caution: "One can shout with his face as well as with his voice. An overly expressive face can drown out other levels of meaning and so can hyperactive gesticulation. Some speakers defeat their purpose by attracting visual and not aural attention." [5] Videotape and mirror can serve not only to encourage bodily action but to remind us of our saturation point.

Eye contact in preaching is not a gimmick. It aids in meeting communication needs to which Malcomson has directed attention. Steadily meeting the eyes of listeners, the preacher goes far toward satisfying their need for one who knows and values their presence, who is attentive to their responses, and who meets them in interactive openness that is ready to receive their contributions to the preaching event. By his eye contact the preacher expresses his need of the listener as a person, not a unit in an audience.

Eye contact, therefore, cannot be simulated. The expedient of the shy and preoccupied, of looking just over the heads of the listeners, or of occasional quick glances in their direction, is worse than useless. The test is not whether we *appear* to look at the listener, but whether we *see* the listener with a clarity and concentration that picks up cues essential to the kind of responsive adjustment in delivery that facilitates the personal relation.

What is at stake is an inner attitude, not a mere gesture of the eye. There is some data which indicates a connection "between visual interaction and desires for domination or warm human contact." [6] Ralph Exline reports his finding that speakers who desire real communion with others look at them significantly more than do those who seek merely to dominate. Yet in a highly competitive situation the tendency is reversed; there, dominators employ the coercive stare, and affiliators seem unwilling to embarrass others by such forceful looks. Perhaps in subconscious realization that this is true, we are drawn to the preacher who meets our eye as he tells the good news, but we resist the preacher who looks most intently at us in the moments when he scolds. We need wise practice of the physical skills that help to carry the message, but still more we need to come to the situation in loving concern for the people that finds genuine expression in even the most subtle movements.

Determining an Appropriate Method

Alternative methods of delivery must be evaluated in terms of their effectiveness in facilitating the personal relationship between preacher and listener, free from the intrusion of the sermon as a third element. Three possibilities are open to us: to read the sermon from manuscript; to commit it to memory verbatim and so to deliver it in verbal perfection; or, in extempore style, to prepare the content carefully but leave the wording to the moment of encounter. Each method has advantages and liabilities.

Reading from manuscript assures accuracy of statement and reduces strain on the preacher. It guards against deviation from the time allotted for the delivery. Some preachers believe they need the protection of a manuscript in controversial situations, as proof of what they said. None of these assets moves far into the realm of personal relations. Verbal accuracy is not personal relationship, and a preacher who sometimes gropes for a word but is personally involved with his listeners is more persuasive than one who is letter perfect and withdrawn. To prepare a manuscript as proof of what was said is to be overcautious; furthermore, a prepared manuscript is hardly proof of what was said. Speakers often depart from their manuscripts; only a tape recording can offer real evidence of what the preacher said.

Yet some preachers can give themselves most fully with the aid of a manuscript. Those who use it well do not read it as the record of what they thought last week; they rethink it in the living present. Most preachers who achieve this difficult feat have previously marked key words and ideas, so that they stand out at a glance; they have read the manuscript so many times that they are thoroughly familiar with its content; and with this preparation they are able to speak it naturally, with maximum attention to their listeners. Those who preach well by this method first write as if they were speaking, and then read as if they had not written. The formula is difficult, and only a few fulfill it.

Of the memorization method little needs to be said. In verbal accuracy and time control, it shares the advantages of the manuscript method. Unlike the manuscript, the memorized sermon leaves the preacher free for maximum bodily participation and eye contact. Yet it sacrifices one of the principal values of eye contact, for the preacher is committed to his memorized pattern and is not free to adapt to cues he reads from the faces in the congregation. For most preachers the strain of weekly writing and verbatim memorization is prohibitive.

The extempore style of delivery (not to be confused with the impromptu!) combines carefully prepared thought with freedom to adapt to the needs of the hour of delivery. All that we have considered in previous chapters—long advance scheduling of themes, gathering of thought and material over a period of months, careful sharpening of the dynamic idea, meticulous outlining, writing and rewriting of the manuscript—can be combined with extempore delivery. Its uniqueness comes at the point where the minister leaves behind his manuscript and all but the most sketchy notes, to speak to the people out of this background but in no set pattern of words and sentences.

The risks of extempore delivery are greater. Choice sentences from the manuscript may refuse to come in the heat of the moment. To speak with as great an economy of words as that of the typed page is difficult; hence control over the time element is not fully assured. Preparation is more exacting; the preacher must have such command of the movement of thought, not only in broad outline but in detail, that he can move through it with certainty.

The advantages of extempore delivery are also great. Detailed preparation combines with freedom to respond to the situation and the people. Whereas preachers who work from manuscript or memorization *may* rethink the sermon at the moment of delivery, the preacher who works in extempore style *must* rethink it in attentive contact with the listeners. For the greater number of preachers this is the method that offers the highest probability of entering into a genuine communicative relationship with a congregation, and the least likelihood of the intrusion of the sermon as a third element.

Every preacher must find the method that best suits his talents and limitations. It would be a violation of personality to attempt to pour all into the same mold. Experimentation with manuscript, memorization, and extempore delivery is a part of finding one's identity as a preacher. In all this, one test is paramount: that method is best which most fully facilitates a relationship of personal communication with the hearer. All other criteria are secondary to this.

Making Spiritual Preparation

The spiritual preparation of the preacher is vital to the relationship. Here again, Malcomson, in his delineation of communication needs, points to what is required. We noted the need for dialogue with someone who brings not only his openness but his own sense of urgency to communicate the message; the need for therapy given by one who—with himself off his hands—can give himself fully to helping us; the need for judgment by one who has earned the right to speak; and the need for one who is committed to others and to the common faith and cause. No one can fulfill such needs without unhurried spiritual preparation.

When the sermon has been prepared, it is still necessary to prepare the preacher. He must get the sermon off the paper and into his mind and heart. His writing and rewriting was part of this process, but now he must reread repeatedly and extract the outline again from the written paragraphs, thus tracing the movement of the essential thought. If he preaches in the extempore style, he may need to verbalize the sermon to the walls of his empty room, assuring himself of familiarity with alternative ways to move through it. He may even find it useful to verbalize for a tape recorder and test himself by the playback. At whatever cost, he must get the written sermon so deeply into his thought and feeling that it has ceased to be a literary piece and becomes the material of oral communication.

Beyond this, he needs preparation in prayer. Preaching is more than intellect; it is spirit. As such, it needs spiritual reality in its preparation. The preacher does not speak in his own right; he is credentialed as a spokesman of his Lord, the living Word. He can be true to that mandate only as he keeps close to his Lord in prayer. The sermon is not secular oratory; it is a part of worship. It will be out of its native air unless it is conceived in worship and drenched with worship in its preparation. The object of preaching is to meet some urgent need of the people, and he will preach with greatest fidelity to that objective who comes to the hour of delivery fresh from intercession for the people and their needs. The preacher can do his best work, not in self-conscious anxiety, but in God-conscious devotion and in loving consciousness of the people; which means he will do his best when he comes to the pulpit from prayer that has freed him from anxiety by putting him and the total need of the hour fully in the hands of God.

Such preparation requires unhurried time. How this is managed will vary with the man and his situation, but such time must be found. Quiet concentration on the message before retiring, and sufficiently early rising to allow more time before going to preach, are not optional but essential. "Cramming" one's spiritual preparation in these last hours has the same doubtful value as "cramming" one's studies for an examination. Authentic final preparation builds on personal growth through the management of time, valid intellectual disciplines, and a steadily cultivated spiritual life. Such growth needs its own concentrated attention and will focus our thought in the final chapter.

PROBES

Two books treat delivery methods in discussions divergent from each other and from this chapter: Ilion T. Jones, *The Principles and Practice of Preaching* (Abingdon Press, 1956), Chs. 11 and 12; and Halford E. Luccock, *In the Minister's Workshop* (Abingdon Press, 1954), Ch. 18. Important matters dealing with the interpretation of the message through oral expression, necessarily untouched in this book, are usefully illuminated in Harold A. Brack, *Effective Oral Interpretation for Religious Leaders* (Prentice-Hall, Inc., 1964).

CHAPTER 17

Growing in
a Communicative Ministry

"The sermon is the preacher up to date," wrote William A. Quayle. "All his life flowers in what he is saying at a given time. No man can say bigger than he is. He can borrow big phrases and tell them; but their vastness is not his." [1] The dictum recalls the little Pauline catechism on what finally lasts. Is it fine sermons? "Prophecies . . . will pass away." Is it religious ecstasy? "Tongues . . . will cease." Is it knowledge? "Knowledge . . . will pass away." What, then, endures? "Love never ends" (I Cor. 13:8). Communicative ministry rests finally on deep reality in life and spirit.

Philosophers, as well as apostles, have known this. "We believe good men more fully and readily than others," said Aristotle, and then added: "It is not true, as some writers assume in their treatises on rhetoric, that the personal goodness revealed by the speaker contributes nothing to his power of persuasion; on the contrary, his character may almost be called the most effective means of persuasion he possesses." [2] A chorus of memorable communicators, joining in that judgment, links the centuries.

This book has tried to focus attention objectively on functions, steadily asking, What does effective communication require us to *do?* That question, however, has often driven us back to the significance of the kind of person the communicator *is:* his openness to interaction, in which he is not assured in advance that his way will prevail, his personal reality confessionally revealed in the "expressive" style, his spiritual fitness as a prerequisite for strong delivery of the message.

A question Quayle asks and answers carves a cameo of this truth. "Preaching is the art of making a sermon and delivering it? Why, no, that is not preaching. Preaching is the art of making a preacher and delivering *that*. Preaching is the art of the man giving himself to the throng by means of voice and gesture and face and brains and heart, and the background of all these, himself. . . . Therefore, the elemental business in preaching is not with the preaching, but with the preacher. It is no trouble to preach, but a vast trouble to construct a preacher." [3] Some implications of that statement require attention as we conclude.

Growing in Intellectual Wholeness

To "construct a preacher"—or any authentic communicative ministry—calls for continuous growth toward wholeness of mind. Though this ministry calls for more than intellect, it is a pathetic thing without that. How can we speak for him who is the Truth if we are incapable of hard, clear thought? What can make us credible in the midst of a knowledge explosion if our thinking is innocent of the relevant facts? Or how can we endure the indignity of exposing our minds to the public gaze, week after week, unless they be decently clothed?

Ordination never made a man worth hearing. Nor did years of professional training. If the breathless advance of learning, the tidal wave of print, and the clash of opinion in the marketplace of ideas did not enforce never-ending diligence in study, the old cost of a worthy opinion would: no man's message is worth more than the price he has paid in disciplined investigation and mature meditation upon it. Last-minute fevered thumbing of sources on a theme may gather impressive materials; it cannot give wholeness to thought about them. The sparkling bits and pieces leave a jagged void around the periphery, where yesterday's or last week's catch-up study ran out of time. The minister whose reading is chiefly for next week's sermon must settle for a mind that becomes a thing of shreds and patches.

Relentlessly the communicative minister must hold the pace of his reading. He cannot keep up with the presses, but a book or two a week is not too much to ask of himself; that pace held across the years—if he chooses with care—can keep his mind respectably ready for its task. Of course, as an honest workman, he will read in the technical fields that inform his craft: a solid theological journal or two, the cream of the new books on the growing edge of Biblical scholarship, some decent conversance with the advance of behavioral and social studies. Only a charlatan would presume to speak professionally on the great human and religious issues without this foundational preparation kept up to date. This is the baseline of his study, not its range.

Human life is his field; and technical writing, essential as it is, gives a bloodless account of human life. What the psychologists explore in the laboratory, or the sociologists survey in the field, the novelists and dramatists relive in experience. Technical studies validate generalizations from masses of data; the enduring literature of the imagination helps us to walk in the shoes and ache with the hurts of individual men and women. The best poets, playwrights, and storytellers observe with eyes perceptive of minute detail and report with empathic imagination through which we gain experience, authentic though vicarious. To read steadily in the best of such literature is to live more lives than our own and to have familiar neighbors in more than our hometown.

"Through literature," wrote John Ciardi, "the voices of mankind's most searching imaginations remain alive to all time. No man is half civilized until those voices have sounded within him. A savage, after all, is simply a human organism that has not received enough news from the human race. Literature is one most fundamental part of that news. One needs to hear Job lift his question into the wind; it is, after all, every man's question at some time. One needs to stand by Oedipus and to hold the knife of his own most terrible resolution. One needs to come out of his own Hell with Dante and to hear that voice of joy hailing the sight of his own stars returned-to. One needs to run with Falstaff, roaring in his own appetites and weeping into his own pathos. What one learns from those voices is his own humanity. He learns what it is to carry about within mortal meat a bulb of brain wired to a brush of dendrites. Until he has heard those voices deeply within himself, what man can have any sizeable idea of himself?" [4]

Or, we might add, what preacher can have any clear conception of the deep humanity of the men and women he addresses? By such reading he can be liberated from the press of the parochial and the constrictions of the contemporary. His sympathies can be quickened, his judgments mellowed, his wisdom fortified by feeling on his own pulse a breadth of experience he could not otherwise crowd into one short lifetime. Together with the biographical writings whose worth we have noted, such literature will steadily contribute to the mind of the growing communicator. Whether or not, in the demands of his ministry and the pace of publication in his technical fields, he can hold the pace sometimes advised, of two books of such literature for every technical book he reads, he will live much in the area of imaginative and humane letters and will be the richer for it.

The first five years out of school set patterns for a whole ministry. Important changes after that are possible but frighteningly difficult. The first five years without the stimulus of classmates and the rigors of assignments harden the habits of intellectual self-discipline or the loss of studiousness among the distractions of the parish. Happy the minister who, on coming from his last full-time academic program, sets himself without delay to a program of studies planned with care and held to with unyielding insistence. The years hold out hope that he can "construct a preacher" by growing a mind.

Establishing Time Control

Hopes of such growth swiftly vanish apart from firm control of one's time. At this point the minister is vulnerable. He punches no time clock. If he is pastor of a one-minister church, he reports to no office where colleagues hold him accountable. Calls from many sources converge upon him. If his study is in his home, household affairs easily spill over from the ends of the business day into its creative hours. More than most men, the minister faces the probability of self-destruction through no great wrong he does, but by the nibbling failure to control his time. He needs at all costs to gain mastery here—by keeping a log of his hour of arrival at work and of the hour and minute of each departure from and return to his desk, or by whatever device will best bulwark his defenses.

Tactfully he can win his people as allies in this struggle. In beginning a pastorate, a minister can set its tone. If he is wise, as well as loving, he will show his people, and tell them plainly, that he wants to be their friend in all joys and sorrows and that he covets their calls upon his attentions and energies in every kind of need. In that context, he can add another concern. "Responding to these highly proper and much-wanted calls," he can say, "is one very important aspect of my work, in which I serve you, one by one. But there is another ministry in which I serve you all at once. That is in my leadership of worship, my teaching and preaching. I am not brilliant enough to do that as well as you deserve to have it done, without considerable cost in weekly study. I want to serve you well, both as individuals and as a congregation. To that end, I can work best by dividing my day. I shall be in my study early in the morning, working toward an effective ministry to the whole congregation, until eleven. The rest of the day—and the night, too, when you need me—belongs to individuals. Please call me at *any* hour, if there is an emergency; but when no emergency is involved, you will help me to be a better minister to all of the people by waiting until eleven o'clock to call."

Not everyone will hear and heed, but many will, and a tone will be set for a pastorate in which loving care of individuals and a growing ministry as a teacher-preacher can thrive together. It is not true that the demands of the parish make concentrated study impossible. These demands are many, and their distractions are real; but they prevail only when the minister has not established his own priorities. In many a parish with multiple programs and pressing needs, the minister serves individuals with care that earns their love, efficiently administers a welter of activities, and yet fences the study hours that support the growing pulpit ministry his people prize. Such ministers know there are separate parts to their work, that each part is important, and that each part must have its allotted time.

Knowing this, they devise means to see that they, not circumstances, control their ministry. They devise such means, for instance, as living by a plotted day: a settled time of early rising; fixed and undeviating hours for study; other times for administration and calling; time for family and friends; and, since early rising is fruitless without proper rest, a disciplined bedtime. Or, to take another example, they devise such means as the "geographical" segregation of study from administration. Doing both from the same desk can be endlessly distracting. One studies with the paper work of administration before him, dividing his attention; then he turns to administrative chores with his books and unfinished sermon in plain view to haunt his mind. Some ministers study at home and do office work at the church. Others place their chair between two desks; when they face the study desk their back is to administration; when they face the administrator's desk their back is to study. Devices vary; the principle of establishing control of one's ministry remains constant and essential.

The struggle need not make the minister a heartless martinet. Scheduled hours can include time for the family. A minister with young children, for instance, may hold to a rule of no evening meetings before eight, giving him opportunity for an unhurried dinner with his family on most nights, and a chance to be with small children until their early bedtime. A minister with older children may plan activities with them, which are entered in his engagement book and honored with the faithfulness accorded other commitments. Family outings and vacations planned and spent together can deepen fellowship. Family time is measured by quality, not quantity. The minister who is otherwise in control of his time and at peace with himself can be fully present with his family when he is with them. The completeness of his presence may give them more in limited hours than absorbed watchers of television or grumpy putterers give their children in twice the time.

Gaining a Strategic Center

Establishing vital priorities, controlling one's time and ministry, being fully present with those one loves—all this presumes a life made whole by its integration around a devotional center. As Richard Baxter declared long ago, "God never saved any man for being a preacher, nor for being an able preacher; but because he was a justified, sanctified man, and consequently faithful in his Master's work." [5] This strategic center of fruitful ministry cannot be taken for granted. It must be faithfully cultivated.

Crucial to the plotted day is provision for prayer. The minister's day can be built on a structural frame of prayer. He can teach himself to greet the morning with his first waking thoughts turned to God in recollection of the Father's presence and with gladness that where God is, there is strength and love. He can take some quiet moments early in the day, in the midst of some such routine as the daily shave, to give up the day and all its affairs into God's keeping. He can remember that it all came from the Creator's hand, and he can give it back to him, thinking through the day's plans and its busy engagements, and committing each to God. As he comes to his morning studies, he can devote the first, freshest hour to Bible study and prayer. As the day progresses, it can be punctuated with mealtime graces and ejaculatory prayers. At its end there can be a review of its activities in prayer that cleanses the wrongs in the bath of forgiveness, draws anxiety from the unfinished by entrusting it to the Father, and faces the morrow in the assurance of his love and guidance. Retiring with some brief word of Scripture to turn over in his mind, the minister can make his last waking thought, like the morning's first, a commitment to the Father's providence.

As a part of this strong framework of his days, the minister guards time to listen for his Lord's word. We have already discussed his devotional use of the Bible and the keeping of a devotional diary, and we need not retrace these steps; we need only recall their importance. The Reformation made much of the incident in the home of Martha and Mary at Bethany (Luke 10:38–42), which speaks a word needed in our time. Martha was "distracted with much serving," as, indeed, are we; but Mary "sat at the Lord's feet and listened to his teaching." "One thing is needful," Jesus said. "Mary has chosen the good portion." Much of our serving is "distracted" and fruitless because we assume we can carry it by our determined energy and native wit—sustained by much coffee and other stimulants—but have not sufficiently "sat at the Lord's feet and listened to his teaching."

We need help from others. Such an athlete of the spirit as Dietrich Bonhoeffer can renew us by his *Letters and Papers from Prison,* with their atmosphere of Bible-reading and prayer that puts his references to "religionless Christianity" in a certain perspective that hasty secularists sometimes miss. And we can grow strong in the company of ageless devotional classics. The minister who has not lived his way through such treasures as Augustine's *Confessions,* William Law's *A Serious Call to a Devout and Holy Life,* Thomas à Kempis' *Imitation of Christ,* Kierkegaard's *Purity of Heart,* Wesley's *Plain Account of Christian Perfection,* the *Little Flowers of Saint Francis,* and the *Theologia Germanica,* shares the impoverishment that goes with spiritual provincialism. Not merely to read, but to pray his way through, such classics is to find the help that giants of the devotional life can share with us.

As Hanns Lilje observed, the possibility of being theological stars is not open to us. There are no star performances. We *find* ourselves spiritually within a *group.* The New Testament knows no saints in the singular; the word occurs only in the plural, as a reminder that the life with God is corporate. The minister's spiritual growth is so nurtured. He lives within the church, not merely as the medium of his professional ministry, but as the matrix of his maturing Christian experience. He worships with the congregation, *praying* the liturgy, as the very breath of his life, not *saying* it as a clerical functionary. And happy is he if he has found some small group with whom regularly to share his most intimate concerns in prayer.

Without a disciplined spiritual life, it is doubtful whether the minister has any goods that are not secondhand to share with his people. His message then becomes a repeating, on the authority of others, of what he knows only by hearsay. He may be a very nice man, and his communication skills may make it all a pleasant exercise; but it has no ring of authenticity. The ministries that have prevailed most influentially with men have always been those most deeply rooted in earnest, habitual, persevering prayer. "The victory may seem to be won whilst we persuade men," said James Stalker, "but it has to be previously won in the place of intercession." [6]

It is not a rhetorical flourish to conclude in remembrance that communication at its best is a work of grace. So long as any notion endures that we must win our way by our own performance, we are tense, self-conscious, unable to enter into the open relationship essential to a real meeting of persons and meanings. He who knows, not as an orthodox formula, but as a deeply felt reality, that our justification is not by our works but by faith in which we cast ourselves utterly upon the Lord can rise to his full potential effectiveness. Freed from himself, from his fears, and from the strained efforts whose tensions block the best he might give, he can come to the communicative relationship as a whole man, his mind stored, his skills prepared, his spirit uplifted, ready to be fully used.

NOTES

Chapter 1. Communication—Basic to Ministry

1. Edward T. Hall, *The Silent Language* (Doubleday & Company, Inc., 1959), pp. 175–176.
2. *Ibid.*, p. 217. The idea is a recurring thesis of Hall's study.
3. Julius Fast, *Body Language* (Pocket Books, Inc., 1971), pp. 136–138.

Chapter 2. Understanding the Communication Process

1. Cf. Aristotle, *The Rhetoric*, tr. by W. Rhys Roberts (with *The Poetics*, tr. by Ingram Bywater; Modern Library, Inc., 1954). The summary, "good character, good will, good sense, other's mind, other's language," is helpfully developed in a short film, *What Changes and Does Not Change in Communication*, produced by the Institute of Life Insurance (Ridgefield, N.J.: Association Films), 13 min.
2. The Shannon-Weaver model was set forth in Claude E. Shannon, *The Mathematical Theory of Communication* [and] *Recent Contributions to the Mathematical Theory of Communication*, by Warren Weaver (University of Illinois Press, 1949). For a helpful exposition, see B. F. Jackson, Jr., ed., *Communication—Learning for Churchmen* (Communication for Churchmen series, Vol. I; Abingdon Press, 1968), Ch. 3.
3. This diagram is based on one given by David K. Berlo, *The Process of Communication: An Introduction to Theory and Practice* (Holt, Rinehart & Winston, Inc., 1960), p. 72.
4. Cf. James D. Glasse, *Putting It Together in the Parish* (Abingdon Press, 1972), pp. 53–56.
5. This diagram is suggested by one contained in Abne M. Eisenberg and Ralph R. Smith, Jr., *Nonverbal Communication* (The Bobbs-Merrill Company, Inc., 1971), p. 13.

Chapter 3. Sharing the Essential Interaction

1. Sydney J. Harris, *Chicago Daily News,* Dec. 17, 1971.
2. *Bell Telephone Magazine,* April, 1971, as quoted by Harris, *loc. cit.*
3. Cf. Clyde Reid, *The Empty Pulpit: A Study in Preaching as Communication* (Harper & Row, Publishers, Inc., 1967), pp. 67–73, for a somewhat different exposition of the seven levels considered here.
4. Studs Terkel, *Division Street: America* (Pantheon Books, 1967), p. 126.
5. Based on a model shown by Gerald R. Miller in his *Speech Communication: A Behavioral Approach* (The Bobbs-Merrill Company, Inc., 1966), p. 73.
6. This diagram is suggested by John W. Riley, Jr., and Matilda White Riley, "Mass Communication and the Social System," in *Sociology Today: Problems and Prospects,* ed. by Robert K. Merton *et al.*
7. David K. Berlo, *op. cit.,* p. 120.
8. *Ibid.,* p. 130.

Chapter 4. Analyzing the Receiver-Interactant

1. Cf. Theodore Clevenger, *Audience Analysis* (The Bobbs-Merrill Company, Inc., 1966), pp. 101–107, for his treatment of the six questions discussed in this section. I am indebted to this excellent book for a number of emphases in this chapter.
2. *Ibid.,* p. 104.
3. S. I. Hayakawa, *Language in Thought and Action,* 2d ed. (Harcourt, Brace and World, Inc., 1964), p. 204.
4. Bill D. Moyers, *Listening to America: A Traveler Rediscovers His Country* (Harper & Row, Publishers, Inc., 1971), p. 11.
5. John Steinbeck, *Travels with Charley: In Search of America* (The Viking Press, Inc., 1962), p. 5.
6. Cf. Merrill R. Abbey, *Preaching to the Contemporary Mind* (Abingdon Press, 1963), pp. 71–74, 159–187, for a more extended treatment of the deriving and use of axioms.

Chapter 5. Learning the Language of Media

1. Marshall McLuhan, "Classroom Without Walls," in *Explorations in Communication, an Anthology,* ed. by Marshall McLuhan and Edmund Carpenter (Beacon Press, Inc., 1960), p. 1.

2. Marshall McLuhan, "Media Log," in *ibid.,* p. 182.

3. Marshall McLuhan, *Understanding Media: The Extensions of Man* (McGraw-Hill Book Co., Inc., 1964), p. 282.

4. *Ibid.,* p. 283.

5. William F. Fore, *Image and Impact: How Man Comes Through in the Mass Media* (Friendship Press, 1970), p. 14.

6. Charles Sopkin, *Seven Glorious Days, Seven Fun-Filled Nights: One Man's Struggle to Survive a Week Watching Commercial Television in America* (Simon & Schuster, Inc., 1968), p. 280.

7. Stanley J. Rowland, Jr., "Crisis in Church Communication," *The Christian Century,* Vol. LXXXV, No. 40 (Oct. 2, 1968), pp. 1240–1243.

8. Fore, *op. cit.,* pp. 33–34.

Chapter 6. Preaching in a Multichannel Milieu

1. Jeffrey K. Hadden, *The Gathering Storm in the Churches* (Doubleday & Company, Inc., 1969), p. 218. Hadden cites a monograph by Richard V. McCann, *The Churches and Mental Health* (Basic Books, Inc., 1962).

2. The three quotations in this paragraph are from Hadden, *op. cit.,* p. 231.

3. Phillips Brooks, *Lectures on Preaching* (London: H. R. Allenson, 1902), p. 5.

4. Berlo, *op. cit.,* p. 67.

5. Leon Festinger, "The Theory of Cognitive Dissonance," in *The Science of Human Communication: New Directions and New Findings in Communication Research,* ed. by Wilbur L. Schramm (Basic Books, Inc., 1963), p. 21.

6. Joseph T. Klapper, "The Social Effects of Mass Communication," in Schramm, *op. cit.,* p. 68.

7. Ithiel de Sola Pool, "The Effect of Communication on Voting Behavior," in Schramm, *op. cit.,* pp. 128–137.

8. Klapper, *loc. cit.,* p. 68.

9. *Ibid.*

10. Cf. Elihu Katz, "The Diffusion of New Ideas and Practices," in Schramm, *op. cit.,* pp. 77–90.

11. Browne Barr, *Parish Back Talk* (Abingdon Press, 1964), gives a discussion of the sermon seminar by one of its chief exponents.

12. As reported in William D. Thompson, *A Listener's Guide to Preaching* (Abingdon Press, 1966), p. 93.

13. Cf. Reuel L. Howe, *Partners in Preaching* (The Seabury Press, 1967), pp. 96–97.

14. Lowell D. Streiker and Gerald S. Strober, *Religion and the New Majority: Billy Graham, Middle America, and the Politics of the 70s* (Association Press, 1972), pp. 139–140.

Chapter 7. Interpreting the Biblical Message

1. Order for the Ordination of Elders of The United Methodist Church. Similar forms can be found in ordination rituals of other denominations.

2. Harry Emerson Fosdick, *The Living of These Days: An Autobiography* (Harper & Row, Publishers, Inc., 1956), p. 95.

3. Will Herberg, *Protestant—Catholic—Jew: An Essay in American Religious Sociology* (Doubleday & Company, Inc., 1955), pp. 14, 236. The stability of this finding is indicated by the fact that, a decade later, the Gallup poll showed the data changed by only four percentage points.

4. Gerhard Ebeling, *Theologie und Verkündigung,* pp. 14 f., as quoted in *The New Hermeneutic,* ed. by James M. Robinson and John B. Cobb, Jr. (Harper & Row, Publishers, Inc., 1964), p. 68.

5. Gerhard Ebeling, *Word and Faith,* tr. by James W. Leitch (Fortress Press, 1963), p. 329.

6. *Ibid.,* p. 331.

7. Walter Kaufman, "I and You: A Prologue," in Martin Buber, *I and Thou,* tr. by Walter Kaufman (Charles Scribner's Sons, 1970), p. 40.

8. *The Upper Room Discipline* (Nashville: The Upper Room, 1970).

Chapter 8. Teaching a Witnessing Church

1. J. W. Stevenson, *God in My Unbelief* (Harper & Brothers, 1960), p. 96.
2. Richard Baxter, *The Reformed Pastor,* ed. by Hugh Martin, Treasury of Christian Books edition (London: SCM Press, 1956), p. 73.
3. Reuel L. Howe, *Survival Plus* (The Seabury Press, 1972), p. 154.
4. Nels F. S. Ferré, *Faith and Reason* (Harper & Brothers, 1946), p. 4. Ferré defines "right religion" as "our fully positive whole-response to the complete combination of what is most important and most real."
5. William E. Sangster, *Power in Preaching* (Abingdon Press, 1958), p. 79.
6. Berlo, *op. cit.,* pp. 176–177.
7. James Joyce, *A Portrait of the Artist as a Young Man* (The Viking Press, Inc., 1944), p. 16.
8. Berlo, *op. cit.,* p. 187.
9. Harry Emerson Fosdick, *Living Under Tension: Sermons on Christianity Today* (Harper & Brothers, 1941), pp. 102–111. Copyright 1941 Harper & Brothers. All quotations from this volume, here and in Chapter 14, are used by permission of Harper & Row, Publishers, Inc.
10. Berlo, *op. cit.,* p. 89. Berlo's somewhat different exposition of the five factors that strengthen learning, which we have treated in this section, is found on pp. 86–91 of his book.
11. James S. Pike, *A New Look in Preaching* (Charles Scribner's Sons, 1961), p. 38.
12. Merrill R. Abbey, "Tapping the Potential of Programmed Preaching," *Church Management,* Vol. XLVII, No. 8 (May, 1971), pp. 22–24, deals with the methodology of such planning.
13. C. H. Dodd, *The Apostolic Preaching and Its Developments* (Harper & Brothers, 1936), p. 17.

Chapter 9. Counseling from a Pulpit Base

1. Fosdick, *The Living of These Days,* p. 94.
2. Edgar Newman Jackson, *A Psychology for Preaching* (Channel Press, Inc., 1961), p. 76.
3. Charles F. Kemp, *Pastoral Preaching* (The Bethany Press, 1963), p. 31.
4. On the two-valued orientation, cf. Hayakawa, *op. cit.,* Ch. 13.
5. David K. Switzer, *The Dynamics of Grief* (Abingdon Press, 1970), establishes this concept of separation anxiety. I am indebted to Switzer for much in the ensuing paragraphs on grief and its treatment.
6. Fosdick, *The Living of These Days,* pp. 211–221.
7. *Ibid.,* pp. 220–221.
8. *Ibid.,* p. 94.
9. Fosdick, *Living Under Tension,* p. 11.
10. *Ibid.,* p. 150.
11. *Ibid.,* pp. 153–154.
12. Fosdick, *The Living of These Days,* p. 99.
13. Edmund Holt Linn, *Preaching as Counseling: The Unique Method of Harry Emerson Fosdick* (Judson Press, 1966), p. 67.
14. Fosdick, *Living Under Tension,* pp. 71–72.
15. Fosdick, *The Living of These Days,* p. 99.
16. *Ibid.,* pp. 94, 97.
17. *Ibid.,* p. 95.
18. Linn, *op. cit.,* p. 55.

Chapter 10. Exploring Innovative Forms of Proclamation

1. Lycurgus M. Starkey, Jr., "Preaching in a Pop Culture," *Religion in Life,* Vol. XLI, No. 2 (Summer, 1972), p. 198.
2. Cf. John Rowan Wilson, *The Mind,* revised ed. (Time-Life Books, 1972), pp. 40–55, for pictorial presentation of this principle.
3. Hayakawa, *op. cit.,* p. 179.

4. Edgar Dale, *Audio-Visual Methods in Teaching* (The Dryden Press, Inc., 1946), p. 39.

5. Ross Snyder, "The Time of Celebration Is at Hand," *The Chicago Theological Seminary Register*, Vol. LVIII, Nos. 4–5 (May–June, 1968), p. 8.

6. *Ibid.*

7. This résumé reflects an aspect of Paul Tillich's thought repeatedly reflected in his writing and speaking; the elements gathered here summarize a portion of his lecture "The Expression of Religion Through Liturgy and the Arts" in the tape series *Pulpit Preaching Past and Present* (Atlanta, Ga.: S & P Cassettes, No. 9).

8. Cf. William D. Thompson and Gordon C. Bennett, *Dialogue Preaching: The Shared Sermon* (Judson Press, 1969), p. 64.

9. *Very Nice, Very Nice,* a film directed by Arthur Lipsett (National Film Board of Canada, 1961), distributed by Contemporary Films, New York.

10. Cf. Thompson and Bennett, *op. cit.,* p. 61.

11. Dennis C. Kinlaw, "Moving Past Homiletics to Innovative Preaching," *The Christian Advocate*, Vol. XV, No. 14 (July 8, 1971), pp. 13–14.

12. *Ibid.*

13. Thompson and Bennett, *op. cit.,* pp. 24–36.

14. *Ibid.,* pp. 36–64.

15. *Ibid.,* pp. 65–72.

Chapter 11. Releasing the Dynamics of the Idea

1. H. Grady Davis, *Design for Preaching* (Muhlenberg Press, 1958), pp. 43–44.

2. James Armstrong, *The Urgent Now: Sermons on Contemporary Issues* (Abingdon Press, 1970), pp. 80–88.

3. Eugene Carson Blake, "A Proposal Toward the Reunion of Christ's Church," in *The Challenge to Reunion,* ed. by Robert McAfee Brown and David H. Scott (McGraw-Hill Book Co., Inc., 1963).

4. Ernest T. Campbell, "The Enigma of Providence," *Pulpit Digest,* Vol. LII, No. 396 (June, 1972), p. 25.

5. Donald M. Baillie, *Out of Nazareth: A Selection of Sermons and Lectures,* ed. by John Baillie (Charles Scribner's Sons, 1959), p. 55.

6. John Knox, *The Integrity of Preaching* (Abingdon Press, 1957), p. 22.

7. *Man's Disorder and God's Design* (Harper & Brothers, 1949), Vol. II, p. 81.

8. Cf. Abbey, *Preaching to the Contemporary Mind,* pp. 159–187, for brief essays sampling the dialectic between Brunner's axioms and texts that speak to them.

Chapter 12. Creating a Communicative Design

1. Davis, *op. cit.,* p. 24.

2. Theodore Clevenger and Jack Matthews, *The Speech Communication Process* (Scott, Foresman & Company, 1971), p. 86.

3. Cf. Ilion T. Jones, *The Principles and Practice of Preaching* (Abingdon Press, 1956), Ch. 5, for another statement of the five principles stated in this chapter. I have reworked Jones's statements and have qualified his fifth principle in the light of communication research.

4. J. Wallace Hamilton, *The Thunder of Bare Feet* (Fleming H. Revell Company, 1964), pp. 101–102.

5. *Ibid.,* p. 102.

6. *Ibid.,* p. 107.

7. *Ibid.,* p. 109.

8. James S. Stewart, *The Wind of the Spirit* (Abingdon Press, 1968), pp. 20–32.

9. David H. C. Read, *Sons of Anak: The Gospel and the Modern Giants: Sermons* (Charles Scribner's Sons, 1964), p. 105.

10. *Ibid.,* p. 107.

11. *Ibid.*

12. *Ibid.,* p. 109.

13. Wayne C. Minnick, *The Art of Persuasion,* 2d ed. (Houghton Mifflin Company, 1968), pp. 260–263.

14. Nathan Maccoby, "The New 'Scientific' Rhetoric," in *The Science of Human Communication,* ed. by Wilbur Schramm (Basic Books, Inc., 1963), p. 49.

15. *Ibid.*

16. *Ibid.*
17. Frederick W. Robertson, *Sermons Preached at Brighton* (Harper & Brothers, 1903), pp. 504–509.

Chapter 13. Achieving Interactive Interest

1. William A. Quayle, *The Pastor-Preacher* (Jennings and Graham, 1910), p. 124.
2. Minnick, *op. cit.*, p. 59.
3. David Frost, *The Americans* (Stein and Day, Publishers, 1970), p. 147.
4. Fosdick, *Living Under Tension*, p. 224.
5. Helmut Thielicke, *Life Can Begin Again: Sermons on the Sermon on the Mount*, tr. by John W. Doberstein (Fortress Press, 1963), pp. 37–38.
6. Minnick, *op. cit.*, pp. 63–64.
7. James S. Stewart, *The Strong Name* (Charles Scribner's Sons, 1941), pp. 251–254.
8. Rudolf Flesch, *The Art of Readable Writing* (Harper & Brothers, 1949), p. 68.
9. Frost, *op. cit.*, p. 158.
10. Edgar Newman Jackson, *op. cit.*, p. 76.
11. *Ibid.*, p. 19.
12. George Arthur Buttrick, *Sermons Preached in a University Church* (Abingdon Press, 1959), p. 13.
13. Wallace E. Fisher, *Preaching and Parish Renewal* (Abingdon Press, 1966), pp. 132, 134.
14. Fosdick, *Living Under Tension*, pp. 51–52.
15. Frost, *op. cit.*, p. 155.
16. Armstrong, *op. cit.*, p. 123.
17. Minnick, *op. cit.*, p. 75.
18. Arthur John Gossip, *The Hero in Thy Soul* (Charles Scribner's Sons, 1933), p. 116.

Chapter 14. Fashioning Substance That Communicates

1. Armstrong, *op. cit.*, pp. 31–32.
2. *Ibid.*, p. 33.

3. *Ibid.*, p. 34.
4. Fosdick, *Living Under Tension*, p. 32.
5. *Ibid.*
6. *Ibid.*
7. *Ibid.*, p. 33.
8. *Ibid.*
9. *Ibid.*, p. 32.
10. *Ibid.*, p. 33.
11. Terkel, *op. cit.*, p. 20.
12. Fosdick, *Living Under Tension*, p. 229.

Chapter 15. Evolving a Communicative Style

1. *Letters*, Nov. 24, 1749.
2. Cf. Ozora S. Davis, *Principles of Preaching* (The University of Chicago Press, 1924), Part II, Ch. 12, as an example.
3. Lecture at Harvard, Nov. 6, 1867.
4. *Lady Holland's Memoir*, Vol. I, Ch. 11.
5. William Strunk, Jr., *The Elements of Style*, revised by E. B. White (The Macmillan Company, 1959), p. 57.
6. Cf. Flesch, *The Art of Readable Writing*.
7. W. Norman Pittenger, *Christ and Christian Faith: Some Presuppositions and Implications of the Incarnation* (Round Table Press, Inc., 1941), p. vii.
8. Jim Gaines, "A Talk About Life and Style with Tennessee Williams," *Saturday Review*, Vol. LV, No. 18 (Apr. 29, 1972), p. 26.
9. Frost, *op. cit.*, p. 216; televised interview quoting Raymond Price.
10. James M. Wall, *Church and Cinema: A Way of Viewing Film* (Wm. B. Eerdmans Publishing Company, 1971), p. 34.
11. Charles L. Rice, "The Expressive Style in Preaching," *Princeton Seminary Bulletin*, Vol. LXIV, No. 1 (March, 1971), pp. 30–42.
12. *Ibid.*, p. 39.
13. *Ibid.*, p. 34.
14. From an unpublished sermon by Robert Koch preached at Irving Park United Methodist Church, Chicago, Feb. 20, 1972.
15. Buber, *op. cit.*, p. 60.

Chapter 16. Getting the Message Heard

1. Knox, *op. cit.,* p. 67.
2. William L. Malcomson, *The Preaching Event* (The Westminster Press, 1968), pp. 15–21.
3. S. E. Asch, *Social Psychology* (Prentice-Hall, Inc., 1952), p. 139.
4. Joost A. M. Meerloo, *Conversation and Communication: A Psychological Inquiry into Language and Human Relations* (International Universities Press, Inc., 1952), p. 36.
5. Eisenberg and Smith, *op. cit.,* p. 97.
6. *Ibid.,* p. 93.

Chapter 17. Growing in a Communicative Ministry

1. Quayle, *op. cit.,* p. 368.
2. Aristotle, *op. cit.,* p. 25.
3. Quayle, *op. cit.,* p. 363.
4. John Ciardi, "Literature Undefended," an editorial, *Saturday Review,* Vol. XLII, No. 5 (Jan. 31, 1959), p. 22.
5. Baxter, *op. cit.,* p. 29.
6. James Stalker, *Imago Christi* (Hodder and Stoughton, 1889), p. 237.

INDEX